PAW PRINTS ON MY SOUL:

LESSONS OF A SERVICE DOG

JANE BIEHL, PHD

Paw Prints on my Soul by Jane Biehl, PhD

Published by JS Publishers

Publishers Cataloging In Publication Data Available Upon Request

DEDICATION

This book is dedicated to my late mother, Katherine Biehl, who insisted I needed a hearing ear dog for many years until I relented. As usual, she was right!

CONTENTS

ACKNOWLEDGMENTS

Thank you to the friends, veterinarians, and family who have loved and cared for Sita and me over the years. Additionally, thank you to the following individuals who have left significant "pawprints" on my life:

Dr. Shruti Trehan, my oncologist and friend, has not only kept me alive but also encouraged me to write about my experiences.

Laurie Lazzaro Knowlton, a wonderful author and special friend, worked many hours with me on this book and believed in me when I did not.

Marlys Staley and the people at Circle Tail provide a fantastic service for many canines and people, bringing dogs to people like me and changing our lives.

Kyla, Kelly, and the team at Happy Tails Books were attentive and helpful throughout the development process of this book.

Last but certainly not least, Sita, my unparalleled companion, has made countless friends and raised awareness about the special role of a hearing-ear dog. She has taught me and others about appreciation and how to live life to the fullest every single day.

INTRODUCTION
By Laurie Lazarro Knowlton, Author

JANE BEFORE SITA

Elementary school can be brutal for children with differences. In the 1950's and 1960's, there weren't social awareness or anti-bullying campaigns. Children were left to defend themselves against cruel peers and unsympathetic adults.

When Jane Biehl entered school in 1956, she had difficulty hearing the teacher. After several months of being physically punished for not listening, it was discovered she had a hearing loss. She wore a huge body hearing aid with a little pouch attached to her undershirt and a cord running up to her ear. Try as she might, Jane didn't fit the norm, and the children were unkind or ignored her. Jane went through seven years of speech therapy to perfect her speech, and even after her hard work, she still had a slight accent and mispronounced certain letters. Already isolated from the other children, Jane mentioned on several occasions that her only friend during school was her speech therapist.

In spite of all of her difficulties, Jane's tenacious spirit got her through school, and she attended college. She shared with me the effects of fatigue from constantly struggling to hear and lip-read. She expressed what it was like to be so exhausted she often went home from school, work, or social outings and collapsed into bed.

Jane worked against the odds and achieved a graduate degree in Library Science. When she applied for a job as a librarian, Jane was asked, "How can you possibly be a children's librarian with your hearing loss?" At that time there wasn't an Americans with Disabilities Act to protect Jane from someone asking her that question. Jane knew she had the skills and the desire to be a good librarian, and she didn't give up.

Jane's enduring spirit and desire to succeed led to her being a librarian, a college professor, a counselor, and a writer. But in spite of all these accomplishments, Jane's vulnerability and frustrations due to her hearing loss began to mount, and fear began to rule her life. After several instances of being startled by maintenance personnel, family members entering her home, water flooding her house from overflowing sinks because she did not hear the running faucet, and a deaf friend being brutally beaten in his own home, Jane knew she desperately needed help. Although she had often thought she couldn't afford to get a trained dog, and that other people needed the skills of a hearing-ear dog more than she did, God had a bigger plan for Jane.

It was then that Jane spoke with a friend who suggested that Jane look into Circle Tail's hearing-ear dogs. The rest unfolds in the heartwarming story of Sita and Jane.

SITA BEFORE JANE

Sita's early history is sketchy at best. She was found wandering alone on the streets of Springfield, Ohio and taken to a county shelter. This particular pound was a place where dogs and cats would be put down after several days if someone didn't claim or adopt them. The shelter estimated Sita's age at two years old.

Every time a person came into the area where the dogs were caged, Sita watched them choose another dog. She was shy and afraid of the strangers. Fortunately, just before her demise, Sita was rescued by a woman from Circle Tail.

Circle Tail doesn't ever put down dogs because they do not have room for them. Each dog is given an evaluation to see if they have the right temperament to be a service dog. Of the dogs rescued, only one in one-hundred make the cut. The ninety-nine that don't have what it takes are adopted out to families who are lucky to get a dog that has had good basic training.

Sita was taken from the shelter by Circle Tail with the hopes of her becoming a service dog. She was cleaned up and evaluated. At first, the instructors at Circle Tail were skeptical because of Sita's timid nature, but one of the trainers saw potential in her. Sita's initial training was in jail with a prisoner, called her handler. When her handler had to return Sita to Circle Tail, he wrote a note to Sita's future partner:

"I received this good-looking, yellowish, sandy-blonde dog with excitement...My mission with her, in the short time I was to have her, was to make her become a better dog.

I set out to teach her how to become a better dog: instead she trained me to become a better person. With a cold private heart, she taught me to open my arms and receive her joyful kisses and embrace her love of life...

I know! It just seems backwards.

If you receive this bright-eyed beauty, I pray she will teach you too as well as she has taught me.

A Humbled Trainer.

Included in his moving letter was a beautiful picture of an adorable, bright-eyed puppy standing tall and proud. Jane later read this letter about Sita on the Circle Tail website. Jane had no way of knowing that it was God's plan to pair them together.

From the prison, Sita went into a foster home where she continued her training to become a hearing-ear dog. Many months passed, and Sita grew from a pink-nosed puppy to a full grown, well-trained service dog.

The day Jane came to Circle Tail for her first experience with a service dog, she was paired with Sita. As they walked the course together, Sita showed Jane how helpful she could be by alerting Jane to sounds, picking up fallen items, and warning Jane about people approaching her. Jane told the director of Circle Tail, Marlys, that she had become attached to Sita, and it would be difficult to continue working with Sita because she had already fallen in love. Little did Jane and Sita know that while they worked together that day, they were being watched to see if they would bond. This book is the story of their journey together.

Help! Fear Is Taking Over My Life

"Do not be afraid, for I am with you."
Genesis 26: 24

The Word tells us not to be afraid, but fear was taking over my life. I was born with a severe hearing loss. Like hearing people, there are certain times that fear is healthy and a subconscious warning. People with all five senses are better able to assess their environment and make safe decisions accordingly.

But as a hard-of-hearing person, I couldn't hear the footsteps of someone following too close or housekeeping entering my motel room. When a captioned television announcement warned of a severe storm approaching, I'd get anxious because I couldn't hear tornado warning sirens.

Then there were the everyday sounds that worried me. When I was sitting at my computer at home, I often didn't hear someone come into the room behind me. Once I spotted the person, I would jump, and my heart started beating as fast as a drum. I dreaded the day it would be a prowler rather than someone who had the key to my place.

Living alone, I would be frightened, and this caused an increase in blood pressure, rapid breathing, and a fast heartbeat. I hated knowing that if only I could hear normally, this would never happen. I was reminded daily that I was vulnerable, and worries about being attacked began to dictate my life.

It took an alarming event for me to take action. I had belonged to a support group for the hard-of-hearing for over thirty years, and I'd had a friend experience a traumatic event. He was in his home and did not have his hearing aids in, so he never heard the thug enter his house. He was severely beaten and robbed.

When I saw this friend's bruised and battered face, I felt terrible for him. But more than that, I knew I had to do something to protect myself. I prayed to God, asking Him what to do, and then I trusted He had a plan.

*The Lord is my light and my salvation - whom shall
I fear? The Lord is the stronghold of my life - of
whom shall I be afraid?*

PSALM 27: 1

❧

Dear God,

**I know You've told us not to be afraid, that You are
always with us. Please help me to know and trust
this. I pray for Your comfort at all times.**

Amen.

❧

DEVOTIONAL TWO:

WHERE TO GO FOR HELP

*I cried to my God for help. From His temple,
He heard my voice.*

PSALM 18: 6

I needed to find a way to receive help before fear overwhelmed me. The suggestion had been made to me several times to get a hearing-ear dog, but I was uncomfortable with the idea of having a canine. My thoughts ranged from "I can't afford one," to "Other people need a dog more than I do," to "I don't have the knowledge or the time to train a hearing-ear dog."

When I told my mother about my friend who had been beaten and robbed, she said to me, "Are you going to get a dog now?" I felt God was giving me a nudge.

Unfortunately, I had no idea where to go for a service dog. A nurse I knew was involved in a hospital dog-therapy program, and she had once mentioned a hearing-ear dog to me, so I contacted her. She e-mailed me about a program called Circle Tail. She also sent an e-mail to Circle Tail recommending me as a potential companion for a hearing-ear dog.

Circle Tail's program is very unique. All of their funding is through grants and donations. Many of the dogs are rescue dogs who are given an opportunity to be of service while being saved from extermination at the same time. Circle Tail's rehabilitation extends beyond the dogs and includes prisoners who become temporary handlers and trainers. Once the initial obedience training with the prisoners/handlers is complete, the dogs are put in foster homes, where they are trained to help individuals with special needs.

The lingo for a service dog is confusing. Technically, a service dog is one that is specially trained to help people with mobility issues and people who use a wheelchair. The dogs can pick up items for their humans, help them get dressed, open and shut doors, and perform a multitude of other tasks. Hearing-ear dogs are trained like Sita to assist a person who is deaf or hard-of-hearing. Seizure dogs alert their companion before the seizure occurs since the dog can sense the halo before the person. Diabetic dogs can warn their partner if their blood sugar is too high or low. The term service dog is intertwined with hearing-ear and other specialized dogs and is the term best known to the public. I usually tell people I have a service dog, and that is what is inscribed on Sita's vest. An umbrella term for all of the above is assistance dogs.

None of these dogs are considered to be therapy or emotional-support animals. They are more highly trained and required to pass rigid tests to be allowed to go all the places service dogs are allowed. For this reason, Circle Tail is extremely careful who receives these intelligent animals.

I filled out the extensive application and submitted three references. A representative from Circle Tail called and asked me if I could afford a dog's veterinary bills. I explained I had just spent a large sum of money on my ill cat, so clearly no expense was too great when it came to animals in my care.

Circle Tail, unlike many similar organizations, does not charge for a service dog. However, the people in charge want to be certain that the dogs will be cared for. I found out later they would call the veterinarian listed on the application, and if the dog or cat presently owned had not been seen for a year, they would turn down the applicant. It costs over twenty-five thousand dollars to train one of these special dogs, and they certainly want them cared for once the lucky recipient gets them. I understood this and passed that hurdle. They told me that the next step was a home visit.

I was a nervous wreck about the person designated to come to my home. The evaluator needs to check out several factors that benefit the dog. Is the house clean and a place a dog would be comfortable? Are there any other dogs in the home? (Circle Tail doesn't allow other dogs because they can distract the service dog from performing tasks for the individual needing the services.) Is there a place for the dog to be able to run nearby? Is there a fenced yard if it is a private home? Does the applicant understand the seriousness of caring for a dog for twenty fours every day? I was worried that my house just wouldn't live up to their standards.

When Karia came to my home, we immediately bonded. She watched me interact with my kitty, who was very ill. She saw my cozy townhouse with room for Sita inside. Since I rented my house, I could not build a fence, but there was a field right across from my driveway for the dog to run and play.

She also explained all the tasks the dog could perform for me. The partnership between an assistance dog and their human is a unique bond. One never calls themselves an "owner" to the dog; rather they are a companion. A human partner spends more time with an assistance dog than any other creature, human or animal. They are together 24/7. The canine accompanies its partner everywhere, including home, school, shopping, and eating out. They travel together on buses, trains, and planes.

The dog often ends up being a person's ears, partner, and best friend. The human must rely on the canine to be alert and keep them safe. Meanwhile, the dog trusts the human to care for them: to provide food, water, and love.

As I listened to Karia, I knew in my heart that God had guided me to the right place. I began to dream of the day I would have a companion. Karia then told me that she would recommend me and said there might be a dog available. I was ecstatic when she left. God had it all planned out for me.

And He who searches our hearts knows the mind of the Spirit because the Spirit intercedes for God's people in accordance with the will of God.

Romans 8: 27

Dear God,

**Thank You for knowing my needs even before I do.
Thank You for guiding me.**

Amen.

DEVOTIONAL THREE:

SITA WENT TO PRISON

*"Each of you should use whatever gift
he has received to serve others."*

1 PETER 4: 10

Once I'd been made aware of the Circle Tail agency, I couldn't stay off their website. I was excited to think there was a remote possibility I would actually receive a dog! I had an application in. Spellbound, I read and reread about their wonderful programs. Circle Tail has a partnership set up with several Ohio prisons where the dogs are trained by the inmates.

Most people can't afford twenty-five thousand dollars to purchase a service dog. However, having the prisoners act as trainers alleviates some of that cost. Because of the inmates' donations of time and the public's donations of funding, Circle Tail doesn't charge the fortunate recipients for the dog.

What a win-win! Rescue dogs that would have been euthanized are alive. The people who desperately need assistance dogs receive them, and prisoners are giving a service, perhaps for the first time in their lives.

This made so much sense to me as I thought about it. Most people don't have the time to devote to training dogs. We are working, going to school, raising families, paying bills, and living life. But prisoners are cooped up, bored with nothing to do. I can only imagine how awful it would be to stare at four walls all day. I would be claustrophobic. Why not have them initiate the obedience training of these dogs while they are inside the prison walls, letting them be of service to others?

What I didn't realize was the impact training a dog would have on the inmates-turned-handlers. While combing through the literature posted by Circle Tail, I read several testimonies by prisoners who'd been positively changed because of their involvement training potential service dogs. The testimonies of the convicts, and their stories about how the dogs impacted and changed them by showing them unconditional love, brought tears to my eyes.

The pictures of the dogs were endearing. One special photo was of a pink-nosed Lab-mix puppy with an inquisitive look. I knew God was working in the lives of people I would never meet but who had a big part in my future.

A person can do nothing better than to eat and drink and find satisfaction in their own toil.

ECCLESIASTES 2: 24

Dear God,

Every single person on earth is able to be of service, even a prisoner. Thank You for the prisoners who assist in training these special dogs. And Lord, please help me be of service to others.

Amen.

DEVOTIONAL FOUR:

VISITING CIRCLE TAIL

"Do not be afraid: do not be discouraged."

DEUTERONOMY 1: 21

I was accepted. I had passed my home visit. What was going to happen next?

I waited eagerly to hear from Marlys Staley, Circle Tail's director. All of our correspondence was via e-mail because I have a hard time hearing on the phone. Finally, I received the message I'd been waiting for. Marlys and I made an appointment for me to come and visit the facility. I wondered about the fact Karia had told me there might be a dog. Marlys didn't mention this to me. When I asked her how long before I would receive a dog, she said the typical waiting period was one-and-a-half to two years.

My heart sank. Here I'd been all excited and ready for a dog only to found out I'd have to wait so long! Karia must have misunderstood about a dog being available. My emotions felt like a roller coaster as I zoomed up and down between excitement to see what the program entailed and disappointment over having a delay.

Circle Tail was a four-hour drive from my house, so I drove down the day before and stayed overnight. I was by myself, and I felt isolated in the hotel. Usually, I traveled with friends or a family member. All kinds of questions ran through my mind. What was going to happen? Would I get a dog or not? What would be demanded of me? Would the dog like me? Was I capable of taking care of an expensive and well-trained dog?

I realized how little I knew about dogs. We hadn't been allowed to keep a dog in the house growing up. My family was a farm family that believed dogs stayed outside. My biggest fear was that I would ruin a perfect dog once I received one. Butterflies fluttered in my stomach for the entire drive down and all through the stay at the hotel. Needless to say, I did not sleep well that night.

The next morning I drove the twelve miles from the hotel to Circle Tail. By now, the butterflies were replaced by my pounding heart; it felt like it was going to burst right out of my chest. Of all the crazy things I had done in my life, this felt like it might top the list. What had I gotten myself into this time?

Once I arrived at Circle Tail, I entered a huge room and stopped inside the door in amazement. The room held at least fifteen dogs with their partners holding their leashes. The teams were going around in a huge circle much like the obedience classes I saw at PetSmart. But this circle was different. There were obstacle courses that the dogs had to navigate. They had to go through tunnels, walk on a thin rail, step on a swaying bridge, and slide under bars. Some of the people handling the dogs had already received a service dog and were bringing it back to the class for practice and training. Some of the humans were foster parents intent on training the dogs for their future partner. Still others were people from the community who'd come in for the obedience classes.

Marlys approached me. She asked a foster mother to bring a dog to me. A beautiful, thin, slightly-built Lab-mix was brought over, and her leash was placed in my hand. My life was about to change forever.

Every good and perfect gift is from above, coming down from the Father of the heavenly lights, who does not change like shifting shadows.

JAMES 1: 17

Dear God,

Do not let me be afraid of change. Life may shift, but You are my constant and always with me.

Amen.

MEETING MY NEW COMPANION

*Show kindness to your servant, for you have
brought him into a covenant with you before
the Lord.*

1 SAMUEL 20: 8

Sita stood tall and proud as she gazed at me. An exquisite expression crossed her furry face as her brows furrowed. She had a look of sweetness and softness that drew me to her. Her face was not flattened like a typical Lab but finely sculptured and dainty looking.

Her nose wasn't the typical black nose seen on most dogs, either, but a sunburned pinkish color. Her face was perfect, except for one little wart on the side which added to her attractiveness. Instead of looking ugly, it gave her a signature look of a movie star.

Sita's most compelling feature was her unusual deep eyes. The color was not quite brown or green but brilliant amber, and they swallowed me in her gaze. As I stared into the beautiful face with those expressive eyes, I was smitten.

Sita and I exercised around the obstacle course for over an hour. She obeyed every command and was eager to please me. Her quiet and calm personality was obvious.

I walked over to Marlys and said, "She's getting tired. And I am getting very attached to her. I do not want to work with her any longer because I will not be able to give her up. I have fallen in love with her. Who does she belong to?"

Marlys smiled and answered, "You now."

Both Marlys and Sita's foster mother, Tracy, had been watching our interactions to see if Sita and I worked well together. It was important to them that I be gentle, yet firm. Sita had been trained to be sensitive to sounds, and if I was too loud or abrupt, I could upset her. It is imperative that the human and the dog have personalities that match. I am easily hurt and do not like people yelling at me, so I understood Sita.

God in his wisdom knew that I worked with both children and adults and did a lot of programs in the community. The private practice where I was employed counseled many foster children who had been abused. I also taught part-time at a community college. When I'd filled out my application for a hearing-ear dog, I wanted Circle Tail to understand that I needed a dog that would be calm and not fluster easily because of all of the interactions that I had on a daily basis. It was like God had read my application. Marlys certainly had and knew how to make the perfect match!

Marlys explained to me that some breeds of dogs look more serious and scary, especially for children. She knew Sita had a soft look that would not frighten the clients I worked with. They had been convinced that Sita would work well with me but wanted to be sure our personalities meshed. Once they'd observed my handling of Sita, they'd decided we were a match. We were about to be forever partners.

My command is this: Love each other as I have loved you. Greater love has no one than this: to lay down one's life for one's friends.

JOHN 15: 12-13

❧

Dear God,

Thank You for the special love that wonderful dogs have for us. Let us be a reflection of Your love with both animals and human beings.

Amen.

❧

DEVOTIONAL SIX:

THE BONDING BEGINS

"For I know the plans I have for you,"
declares the Lord.

JEREMIAH 29: 11-13

I had fallen in love with Sita from the second I'd gazed into her deep amber eyes and looked at her sweet expression. Unfortunately, Circle Tail's first opening for the intense training required that we wait three long weeks. I was disappointed I couldn't bring her home right then.

Finally, while driving the lengthy way to Cincinnati to pick up my new companion, I reflected on the beautiful creature that was to be a part of my life 24/7 while butterflies fluttered in my throat. I compared myself to a parent waiting with bated breath to adopt a child. I knew I was in love with her, but would she be in love with me?

I stayed at a nearby hotel several miles from Circle Tail. I did not sleep much that night. I was worried about the next evening. I would be bringing Sita back to the room with me, and from then on both of our lives would be different.

The next morning, I eagerly drove the twelve miles to Circle Tail and entered the large room where the dogs were trained. Sita was lying quietly next to Marlys. She jumped up, ran over, and started jumping up and down. Although this was not permitted, Marlys let it go. She said she'd immediately sensed that the bonding had begun. I petted Sita and exclaimed, "She remembers me!"

Marlys smiled. "It looks that way."

Sita and I were meant for each other, and God knew that.

To my relief, Sita and I were not alone. Another young, deaf, vivacious woman named Juanita was being partnered with her beautiful Shih Tzu, Hinkle. Juanita had a constant smile on her face, boundless energy, and a great sense of humor. I liked her immediately, and we would constantly sign to each other. Juanita was allergic to dogs, so Circle Tail had trained a smaller, hypoallergenic breed to be Juanita's ears.

Marlys gave us several ideas how to cement the bonding. One important task was to feed the dogs out of our hands for the next two weeks. I followed all of her directions and felt certain that we were bonding beautifully.

About six months after I had Sita at my side, an amazing event happened. I was sitting with a friend in a local restaurant near my home. A woman came over to me and asked where Sita had been trained. I told her, and she said she knew it had not been at the local place because Sita was so well-behaved. I had heard from several different people that this training center did not have a good reputation.

The next statement, however, floored me. "I have worked with service animals a great deal. That dog never takes her eyes off you. The bonding you have is incredible. How long have you had her?"

When I answered six months, it was her turn to be astounded. Sita and I were meant for each other, and God knew that.

Two are better than one, because they have a good return for their labor. If either of them falls down, one can help the other up. But pity anyone who falls and has no one to help them up.

Ecclesiastes 4: 9-11

❧

Dear God,

Thank You for this special gift of Sita. Please let our bond be unbreakable, and may I always live up to her trust.

Amen.

❧

DEVOTIONAL SEVEN:

BREAKING DOWN BARRIERS

*"Who is this that obscures my plans with words
without knowledge?"*

JOB 38:2

I discovered early on there was more to having a service dog than just bonding. The next three days of training were as hard as any workshop or doctoral class I had ever experienced.

Marlys started our training by explaining the laws about the American with Disabilities Act as they pertained to service dogs. I made the mistake of thinking this would be a review for me since I'd taught college classes on the ADA. However, it was important that I learn exactly what the law stated about taking Sita into public places such as restaurants, stores, and on public transportation. Churches and private clubs were the only places that legally could bar Sita from entry.

Little did I know I was going to use this knowledge sooner than I had anticipated. Just two days after Marlys's ADA class, I readied Sita and me to check out of the hotel. I packed to go home and loaded up my car. Since I was not used to having a dog, I accidentally left her service dog vest in the room.

The door to my room was locked when I returned. I saw a hotel employee and asked him to please unlock the door. He did not speak much English and kept repeating, "No dog. No dog."

Patiently, I told him several times that we had been there for four evenings, Sita was a service dog, and I needed her vest.

He kept insisting he could not let me back in the room. To my surprise, Sita got in front of me and began to emit a soft bark. She is not allowed to bark under any circumstance, but she knew it was her job to protect me.

I think he finally let me in because of Sita. She was not threatening in any way or moving towards him, but she was making sure he did not get any closer to me.

I grabbed the needed item and left. Just as I entered the hall, a woman who must have been his supervisor appeared. She scowled at us. I looked at her triumphantly with Sita's vest snapped on her back, which said, "Service Dog, Do Not Pet!"

I stated, "This is a service dog. We are allowed here. We have both been staying here for the last four evenings."

Her dirty look bore into my back as I walked down the hall with Sita at my side. I realized that Sita was going to bring new complications into my life, but she would always be there for me. I knew that God gave me this dog as part of a plan to assist me.

"For I know the plans I have for you," declares the Lord, "plans to prosper you and not to harm you, plans to give you hope and a future."

JEREMIAH 29: 11

❧

Dear God,

Thank You for the wisdom of the ADA laws that protect the rights of persons with disabilities.

Amen.

❧

TRAINING ME

Humble yourselves before the Lord, and
He will lift you up.

JAMES 4: 10

I had more immediate concerns, however, than the ADA. I was being instantly humbled by how much I had to learn.

At that time, Circle Tail had a very rustic training center with no indoor plumbing. The only bathroom on the premises was a port-a-potty. During a class break, I politely excused myself to trudge outside.

I gazed at the port-a-potty and realized immediately that I had a problem. The bathroom was small, and there was barely room for one person, much less for a person and a dog. As I considered my options, they appeared limited. I couldn't leave Sita outside because she might run away. I couldn't take her in the bathroom with me because it was too small. Obviously, I couldn't sit there with the door open, holding Sita's leash because the bathroom was located near a driveway with people driving back and forth all day long.

I was too embarrassed to go back and explain to Marlys on my very first morning of training that I was unable to figure out such a simple task as answering nature's call.

Sita impressed me with her patience. She stood quietly and waited expectantly for the next command. No doubt her doggy brain was wondering why I was standing there with her leash in my hand and saying nothing.

Then the light bulb suddenly went on in my brain as I looked down at Sita's leash. I could go into the port-a-potty and slide the leash under the door. I was able to leave her safely outside while the door was shut with me inside and holding her leash so she did not bolt. I began to realize that this might be the first of many situations I would be facing trying to figure out what to do with Sita. There really wasn't a rulebook for these everyday dilemmas.

I thanked God for His gift of common sense, knowing that Sita and I were going to have a great future figuring out everything together!

Humility is the fear of the Lord; its wages are riches and honor and life.

PROVERBS 22:4

Dear Lord,

Help me to use my common sense and patience to face whatever challenges are before me with my loyal companion by my side.

Amen.

DEVOTIONAL NINE:

LEARNING HOW TO TRUST

Trust in the Lord with all your heart and lean not on your own understanding; ...and He will make your paths straight.

PROVERBS 3: 5-6

There is no way anyone can prepare you for the way your life changes when you become a companion with a service dog. I knew it was going to be different. I hoped it was going to be a bond made in heaven, but I never expected it to be so stressful.

Marlys taught me that when we went out to eat, "Sita can sit, stand, or lie on her blanket, which is named her place."

On our first night out together without a trainer, we walked into a busy restaurant. Entering with a large Labrador retriever in tow was a whole new experience for me. Sita wore her vest that said, "Service Dog, Do Not Pet." I looked around for a booth or table that had room for a blanket, a Lab, and me.

My new set of ears bumped me whenever a server came, a phone rang, or there was any other unexpected sound such as a baby crying. This was a good thing, but it was new to me, and it took some getting used to.

I was acutely aware that people were staring at me. I am positive many of them did not understand why I had a dog since I was not in a wheelchair or blind. One person actually asked me if I was training the dog. Little did I realize how many times I would be asked this question in the future.

When we returned to the hotel, I faced another dilemma. I didn't know whether to allow Sita on the bed with me or to make her stay on the floor? Was she a pet without her vest on or was she still working? She stared at me with her gorgeous eyes.

It was obvious she wanted to be in bed with me. I decided to allow it since bonding was so important. After all, I rationalized that Marlys had suggested we feed the dogs by hand for the first two weeks to help with our bonding. So why couldn't she sleep with me? I took one look at Sita, and she jumped up and cuddled next to me.

We survived our first evening together! When we went to breakfast, I had absolutely no idea how to proceed. It was a buffet. I could not take her through the food options and hang onto her leash while juggling a plate. I was afraid to leave her at the table without me.

I finally decided she was a trained dog and guessed that she would stay on command. So I directed her to the place on the floor and used the command "Stay."

I walked over to the buffet and kept looking back. Sita was sitting there with her gaze intent upon me. Her intelligent and sensitive eyes never once left me. She sat still as a stone in the park.

I returned with my breakfast and praised her, giving her a treat. She lay down obediently and continued to watch me. When I went back to get a refill on my coffee, Sita watched and waited quietly until my return.

I realized then the incredible patience this dog possessed. I was making all of our experiences harder than I needed to. I needed to relax and trust her. Trust that she would stay in place. Trust that she would not misbehave. Trust that she would follow my commands. Trust that God was in control.

When I am afraid, I put my trust in You.
PSALM 56:3

Dear God,

Please help me to trust Sita, and most of all, in You who would never betray me.

Amen.

DEVOTIONAL TEN:

OUR LEARNING CURVE

Your words have supported those who stumbled;
You have strengthened faltering knees.

JOB 4:4

The people at Circle Tail not only taught us our dog's commands and ADA laws, they also instructed us on how to bathe, clip nails, and groom our dogs. Juanita and I looked at each other and realized we had more to learn than the dogs!

Juanita and I met with Marlys the second day of training. That afternoon, Sita's foster mother went with us to a huge discount center near Circle Tail. We must have looked like a dog parade. Imagine a tiny Shih-Tzu with a beautiful, petite young woman, a large yellow Lab with a tall. plus-size woman, and a trainer all in a line. We tied the leashes to the shopping carts and moved through the store looking for beds for our dogs.

At the end of one aisle, Juanita signed to me "You are so lucky you have Sita."

I looked at Hinkle, who was doing his job perfectly. "I know. I love her. But why am I luckier than you? Hinkle is great too."

Dismayed, she explained, "Sita is big, and people can see her. They are running over my dog!"

Sure enough, when we reached the end of the aisle and started to turn into the next one, Hinkle was so small people did not see him. He was in danger of being squished by the fast-moving carts.

The preoccupied people, intent on getting their Saturday shopping done, were pushing their carts much too fast. Several people nearly ran into Sita and me at the blind spot around the corners. However, when they saw her large size, they would move around her.

It seemed that even the simplest everyday activities like shopping required a whole new mindset. Now I had to shop, watch out for other shoppers, and try to be aware of what Sita was trying to tell me. As my mind wandered to my schedule in the upcoming week, my stomach began to ache. I had been subpoenaed to appear in court for a client of mine two days after I returned home. What would I be up against taking a dog to court?

Marlys warned me that I'd have to do a lot of educating of the public when I went back home. I worried as I thought about all the places I went and tasks I did on a daily basis. How was I going to keep Sita obedient and well-trained when I was floundering trying to relearn everything I did? Sita was now an extension of me. My personal space doubled with Sita. I had many new adjustments to make and even more changes when we got back to our home.

I knew I was going to need God's wisdom and strength to conquer life's new challenges. But I also knew I was committed to my new companion, Sita, and we would find a way with God's help.

I can do everything through Him who gives me strength.

PHILIPPIANS 4:13

❧

Dear God,

Thank You for helping me to learn to meet new challenges, go to new places, and educate people about a service dog.

Amen.

❧

DEVOTIONAL ELEVEN:

Sita's Gifts

*Follow the way of love and eagerly
desire gifts of the Spirit. 1*
Corinthians 14:1

The day after I brought Sita home, we went to visit my mother, who was living in a nursing home. I marveled at both Sita's gentleness and the light in my mother's eyes when Sita entered the room. Mom was standing with a walker. Sita instinctively knew my mother was unsteady on her feet.

I told Sita to, "Say hi." That is the signal to greet someone.

Sita did not bound up to Mom or push. She slowly approached and then gently nudged Mom. Tears filled my eyes as I watched my new companion and my mother together.

"I am so glad you finally got yourself a service dog." My mother settled into loving on Sita. "This dog is such a sweetheart."

Sita and I visited Mom at least five times a week. We would go down the hallway to her room, and Sita would run inside and then stop short of my mom like she was making sure to be extra careful with her.

Sita fast became a favorite of the staff and other patients in the nursing home. I'd take Sita out of vest, and she instantly acted like a therapy dog. The residents loved petting her, and the staff all knew her by name.

Sita had not trained to be a therapy dog, but she seemed to instinctively know how to behave. If someone approached her in a wheelchair or walker, she immediately slowed down, approached the person gently, and allowed them to stroke her as long as they wished.

It never ceased to amaze me, the effect Sita had on everyone who met her. I often watched as Sita walked down the hall with her head up high. It was like watching a wave of joy light up each person's face.

The staff began to ask me if she could visit certain people. One staff person whispered to me that there was a veterinarian who desperately missed his animals and would I please be sure Sita went in to see him. He knew all the places to rub and stroke her, and my throat tightened as I watched this man who'd taken care of dogs his whole life had one to spoil now.

Sita also provided therapy to the staff. Working in a nursing home is very hard, both physically and emotionally. The staff becomes attached to the patients they care for, only to eventually lose them. Many times during my visits to my Mom, the staff members would stop their duties and pet Sita. Their faces always brightened, and their demeanors became more relaxed.

Sita had been trained by Circle Tail, the foster mother, and a prisoner to be a service dog. But her great personality, loving nature, and wagging tail also served her well as a therapy dog. God had truly given not only me, but so many others, a wonderful gift.

Honor her for all her hands have done, and let her works bring her praise at the city gate.

PROVERBS 31: 31

❧

Dear God,

Thank You God for the gifts that You have given us. Please let me be as kind and gentle with everyone as my loving dog is.

Amen.

❧

DEVOTIONAL TWELVE:

LIVING BY THE RULES

Hear, Israel, and be careful to obey so that it may go well with you...

DEUTERONOMY 6: 3

One of Sita's favorite people at the nursing home was LuAnn, who worked at the receptionist desk. LuAnn always kept treats for visiting dogs in a special drawer. Sita was just tall enough to reach the desk. She would place her front paws on the desk, and LuAnn would give her a bone.

This all looked very cute until I took Sita to a pharmacy where she placed her front paws on the counter. The pharmacist did not think it was funny, and I was horrified.

I still had a lot to learn about service dogs. One thought about dog training is that if you allow the dog to do something in one place, they think they can do it everywhere. They are not able to transition behavior from one location to another.

After our visit to the pharmacy, I never allowed her to put her paws on the counter again. She had to go around the desk, and LuAnn would hand the bone to her. Sita would eagerly eat her little bone, and LuAnn would pet her. Then we would go on to see my mother.

On one occasion, Sita and I missed going to see mom for several days because we were out of town. When we returned, Sita became very excited as we approached the building. She realized she was close to LuAnn and her treat. I entered the large foyer with Sita, and I dropped the leash. Sita saw LuAnn, and she took off like a rocket.

What I didn't realize was that the automatic doors did not open as fast as Sita moved, and she slammed into them. I gasped as Sita was knocked back on her haunches. She then picked herself up and hurtled through the doors, which by then had opened. I scrambled after Sita to see if she had been hurt. Thank goodness she was fine. But again, I should have kept Sita with me until we reached the desk.

There was a problem, however. Sita had knocked the doors off the track. The doors would not automatically open or close but stayed partially open. I was horrified that Sita had broken the doors of the nursing home facility!

LuAnn laughed and said, "Wheelchairs do it all the time. I will have the maintenance man fix it. No one will know."

I began to understand that Sita's training helped to keep her safe, and I needed to observe the rules. I thought about how God gave us the Ten Commandments to follow and that I was grateful for His wisdom.

*"Follow my decrees and be careful to obey my laws,
and you will live safely in the land."*

LEVITICUS 25: 18

❧

Dear God,

**Help me to remember that the life rules You've
given us and the rules given to Sita are put in place
to help us be safe and live the best life.**

Amen.

❧

DEVOTIONAL THIRTEEN:

SITA AND THE COURTHOUSE

*Cast all your anxiety on Him because
He cares for you.*

1 PETER 5: 7

My birthday didn't have an auspicious beginning. Butterflies fluttered all over my stomach, and my throat was parched. For the first time in my entire life I had been subpoenaed to appear in court.

I had counseled a young girl for several years, and a nasty custody battle was being settled with seven different attorneys fighting over her future.

My nervousness worsened because I had just brought Sita home only two days earlier. My supervisor at the practice had intervened on my behalf and warned the court I would be bringing her. For one anxious second, I even said to my kind supervisor, "Maybe I should not bring Sita this time."

Her wise answer was, "You and Sita are a team now. Bring her!" This statement from a psychologist who knew me well resonated with me many times after this, as I often reminded myself that we are a team.

The day I was to appear in court, I got lost and went to the wrong building. Fortunately, I had allowed plenty of time and finally entered the correct place.

I eyed the security entrance warily. There was the usual metal detector and a conveyer belt to place my purse. I had flown frequently, so this was not new to me. However, I had never had my companion.

My uncertainty must have shown on my face as I warily stopped to contemplate what to do next.

The guard ordered me to place Sita on the conveyor belt. I blanched and stared at him wild-eyed. I had been taught to always listen to someone in authority, and his uniform intimidated me. I was trying to figure out how to hoist this large dog onto the conveyor belt without hurting her. I envisioned Sita's panic as she went moving through the x-ray machine and away from me.

He then laughed and said, "I'm kidding. She can go through." I breathed again and realized I did not have to take Sita or myself quite this seriously!

After sitting in the waiting room for what seemed like forever, the court attorney approached me. "You don't need to testify because your notes were so complete. That little girl was lucky to have you as her counselor."

I thanked her and turned to leave. I wanted to go celebrate my birthday and have lunch with my mother before I went to the office.

The attorney held out her hand. "The magistrate wants to meet you. Well, actually, she wants to meet your dog. I will take you to her."

I followed the attorney through hallway after hallway, and we entered an empty courtroom. I took Sita out of the vest. The magistrate ran over to pet Sita, and like most people, fell in love with those engaging beautiful eyes. Sita behaved beautifully. She waited until I removed her vest before allowing the magistrate to interact with her. After all, I wasn't about to tell a stern woman in robes not to pet my companion! She stroked Sita, and the dog lifted her paw when she asked her to shake. I did not even know Sita knew this command! The two became fast friends.

As we left the courtroom together, I began to realize that God and this wonderful dog would take me on adventures I had never dreamed of.

*Therefore, if anyone is in Christ, the new creation
has come: the old has gone, the new is here!*

2 Corinthians 5: 17

Dear God,

**Help me to welcome all the new adventures I am
going to have with my partner and most of all let
me lighten up and keep a sense of humor!**

Amen.

DEVOTIONAL FOURTEEN:

FIGURING OUT WHAT I NEEDED TO FIGURE OUT

For great is your love, reaching to the heavens; Your faithfulness reaches to the skies.

PSALM 57: 10

I knew when I was partnered with Sita she would do all the routine tasks for me that hearing-ear dogs are noted for. She had been taught to alert me when the telephone rang, when the doorbell was punched, or when the smoke alarm sounds.

A hearing-ear dog doesn't know the difference between a harmless sound and a dangerous one. The dog's job is to "bump" and then point towards the sound she heard. It is up to me to watch her carefully, look in that direction, and figure out if I need to get out of the way or if the sound is innocuous. This opened up a whole new world of sounds in my environment.

Someone asked me, "What did you do before you had Sita? She has made you aware of so many dangerous situations."

My reply was, "I must have kept the guardian angels busy. They tired of so much work, so they sent Sita to me!"

The first week I brought her home, I realized what she could do for me. Sita was lying peacefully on the couch and appearing to be asleep. Without warning, she jumped off the couch, bumped me, and ran to the door. I followed her and did not see anything.

We settled again. I watched television, and she closed her eyes. Again she jumped up, nudged me, and ran to the door.

My townhouse had an outside patio which led to the carport where I keep my car. I could not see anything but noticed that it was raining quite heavily. I kept peering out into the darkness. Other than a rainstorm, I saw nothing. I was new to having the dog alert me, and I figured the storm was bothering her sensitive ears.

I could not hear the wind blowing outside, so I figured nothing was wrong. I returned to my couch. A third time she gently hit me with her nose and ran to the door. Patiently, I followed her, and this time I turned on the patio light. I still could not see anyone at the door and could not imagine what was disturbing her. I told her "it was okay" which is her cue to settle. She obediently went to sleep, and I thought nothing more about these three incidents.

The next morning. I put Sita on leash and went outside. I walked out in the sunlight and realized the wind had been so powerful that every piece of my patio furniture was upside down!

It looked like I needed training more than Sita did. I decided I shouldn't ever ignore her again. I needed to be intelligent enough to listen to her! She could hear what I could not. Just because I couldn't directly see what the problem was did not mean that it was not there. I needed to have faith in her training.

I realized that it is the same with our faith in God. We don't always understand our situation, but God does.

Now faith is confidence in what we hope for and
assurance about what we do not see.

Hebrews 11: 1

Dear Lord,

Sometimes I have issues with trust, even with my dog. Let me trust that she is attempting with all her being to keep me safe. And let me know You are, too!

Amen.

DEVOTIONAL FIFTEEN:

SITA, MY FURRY GUARDIAN ANGEL

*The angel of The Lord encamps around those who
fear Him, and He delivers them.*

PSALM 34: 7

The patio furniture was just the beginning of the amazing sounds Sita introduced me over the next several years together.

The car is full of noises that hearing people never think about missing, but Sita let me know by her bumping. Sita always sits in the back seat. I bought extenders that fit between the back of the front seat and the front of the back seat, so she could lean forward and nudge me if she heard something.

Obviously, the first sound she needed to learn to alert me to was a siren. I worked on training her by keeping treats in my cup holder. When an ambulance passed by, I would tell her to bump me and then reward her.

I couldn't hear the dinging sound in my old car which told me I'd left my lights on. She'd let me know, so I did not run down the battery. This same car used a beeping noise to tell me when I'd left my keys in the ignition. Again, this wonderful dog was my alerter, and I always remembered to put my seatbelt on because she let me know.

Sometimes the sounds are funny ones. One time I was driving, and she repeatedly bumped me. I knew there was something bothering her and continued to look around. I could not find a siren anywhere or see any alerts on my dashboard. After driving for several minutes, I was finally able to hear the faint sound of church bells. She heard them long before I did and was letting me know.

The most dramatic story, however, occurred shortly after I received her. Marlys had instilled in me during training that these dogs had a sixth sense. The usual reason the service dogs and humans do not work well together is that the human corrects the dog when the canine is doing his or her job. She cautioned me not to correct her unless I was sure she was not trying to tell me something.

We were in a busy parking lot, and I gave Sita the command to enter my car. Instead of jumping in obediently, as usual, she sniffed the car next to me. At first, I was going to correct her. Then I thought maybe someone was in that car! I pulled her to my car just in time to see a PT cruiser peel out of the spot where she had been sniffing. We both would have been hit if we had remained where we were. My heart pounded in my chest as I praised her for letting me know the motor was running in the PT Cruiser. I knew then that Sita, my guardian angel, had arrived to watch over me and keep me safe.

But not a hair of your head will perish.

Luke 21: 18

Dear God,

Thank You, Lord, for this wonderful guardian angel who works so hard to keep me safe. I know she was sent directly from You to me.

Amen

DEVOTIONAL SIXTEEN:

A BUSY FIRST MONTH

*Let the wise listen and add to their learning, and
let the discerning get guidance.*

PROVERBS 1: 5

Sita has also let me know when I could get into trouble with my big mouth. The second evening I had her, she proved this to me.

I was working two jobs and had been out of town for training with Sita. After getting off work, I decided at midnight to go grocery shopping for some items I desperately needed. I believed I'd be safe with my dog.

I bought a few things, and we exited the store. I had anticipated very few people in their parking lot at this hour and was correct. The huge parking area was virtually deserted, except for one car, which had parked so close to me I could not get into the driver's side of my own vehicle without entering sideways.

I could not believe anyone would be so thoughtless that they would park that close when there was an entire parking lot available. I turned to see another person behind me, who had just walked out of the store towards her car.

Tired and exasperated from a long day, I called out to the woman and said, "Can you believe anyone would be so stupid to park like this?"

The woman answered, "Do you need me to move?"

"Oh, no. You're fine!" I exclaimed. This woman I was addressing had parked several spaces away. "It is this car!" I gestured to the one hugging mine.

I was so busy talking, I did not realize Sita was bumping me and trying to tell me something. She then jumped and placed her front paws on the trunk of the errant car parked next to me.

I gave her the command to get into my car from the passenger side since there was no room for her on the driver's side. I delicately entered sideways. Once I got settled and fastened my seatbelt, I turned to see a woman sitting in the car that was parked so tight. She was chomping on a hamburger and glaring at me. I drove away shaking my head, partly because of her thoughtlessness and partly at my own ignorance in not realizing that my dog had been attempting to keep me out of trouble. She'd tried to let me know someone was in that car! Sita's warning made me stop and think. I was not proud of the way I had acted, and it was not the guidance God would have given me.

About a month later, I was caught in bumper-to-bumper construction in front of my house. I could not move since everything had been reduced to one lane, and the police were guiding traffic.

Sita whined desperately in the back seat and paced back and forth. I looked around to see what bothered her. She refused to stop. I strained my neck to see what could possibly be wrong. To my utter astonishment, there was a man operating a crane. The boom part of the crane hung directly over my car.

My spine tingled because there had been several accidents where cranes had fallen and killed people. Now I was nervous and couldn't wait for the policeman to wave me through. Finally, the car ahead of me moved, and I was able to get out from under the crane. Immediately, Sita settled down because she knew I was safe. Sita opened up a whole new world of sounds to me because of her constant attentiveness. I had a lot to learn!

"Listen! Listen to the roar of His voice, to the rumbling that comes from His mouth."

Job 37: 2

❧

Dear God,

Most animals have stronger senses of smell and hearing than we do. Let us learn to treasure all Your creatures and their God-given talents. And to help us control our exasperation over petty little things.

Amen.

❧

DEVOTIONAL SEVENTEEN:

JOB WELL DONE!

So that the servant of God may be thoroughly
equipped for every good work.

2 TIMOTHY 3: 17

It is very difficult to explain to someone who can hear well how much a dog can help their partner feel safe and a part of the outside world. In the next few months, Sita proved to me repeatedly that she was going to open up a whole new world of sound to me. Not only that, Sita doesn't do the bare minimum when she performs a task for me. She is always trying to do more. Sita knows her job and doesn't just bump me to let me know there are noises. She also turns her head and points at any unusual sounds. I learned early on not to ignore any motions of that beautiful head.

I was shopping at a busy flea market where it was windy and cold. I stopped the cart and turned to give Sita the command to enter the back seat of my car. Instead of obeying, she turned around quickly. I followed her gaze just in time to see my shopping cart rolling down an incline. I was able to catch it before it smashed into another car at the bottom of the hill. It would have been a disaster, a dented car, and a pile of broken glassware.

Two situations that exemplified Sita's dedication happened while I was teaching in my classroom. The school is located in a busy area. Sita jumped up and bumped me. I turned to see the faces of the students with their mouths dropped in amazement. I couldn't hear anything and asked them what was happening. They told me that a siren had sounded outside the window.

Still another time she helped me when she looked like she was sound asleep. Suddenly, she got up and bumped me and stood next to me for a while. After petting her and trying to calm her, I sternly told her to settle.

The speaker for the class that day came up to me later and explained there was a helicopter overhead, and she was staying there until I heard it or gave her my "It's okay" command to relax again.

Both my students and I have been surprised by her constant vigilance in class. Sita could appear to be sound asleep. However, if a student attempted to leave class early or come in late, she immediately jumped to her feet and nudged me. The students soon discovered that just because their instructor is hard-of-hearing that they were not going to get away with much at all!

I have a favorite bookstore and coffee shop Sita and I visit frequently. Once or twice, people have come up behind me and startled me. This is a common complaint by people who are deaf or hard-of-hearing. If the person does not come around to the front to face us or tap our shoulder, we are startled because we didn't know they were there.

Sita began to get up and move behind me for no apparent reason instead of lying beside me. I did not understand why at first, and my inclination was to correct her. Eventually, I comprehended that someone had passed by behind me, and she knew I did not hear them. She figured this out entirely on her own. Now she bumps me when someone approaches me in a restaurant, cashier lines, and even in class. If someone at the next table begins to talk to me and I do not hear, she bumps me to let me know.

I realized now that God sent a safety net in Sita. Being observant and watching me closely, she comprehended all the sounds around me I never knew existed before. She opened up a whole new world of sound and people to me.

Do we tend to do just the basic parts of a job when asked by our supervisor? When we are tired, do we cut short a prayer? When we should be helping someone, do we opt out? We need to be willing to give more of ourselves.

Whatever you do, work at it with all your heart, as working for the Lord, not for human masters.

COLOSSIANS 3: 23

Dear God,

Thank You for making me feel safe and alerting me to sounds I never heard before. I am blessed by this wonderful angel You sent me. Like Sita, help me go the extra mile in service to others.

Amen.

DEVOTIONAL EIGHTEEN:
REUNITED WITH NATURE

But be glad and rejoice forever in what I will create.
ISAIAH 65: 18

In my busy schedule, I had forgotten about the joy of communing with nature. Sita reintroduced me to the wonderful world of being outside. I was raised on a farm and loved working in the fields, driving a tractor, and walking along looking for arrowheads and stones. However, after I moved away, I did not spend enough time outdoors until Sita became my companion. Every evening after work, I would take her for a walk around the block where I lived. Then it dawned on me that there was an elementary school playground within walking distance. I decided this would be the perfect place for us to visit.

This is not a typical place for children to have recess. The parents have invested a lot of money on expensive equipment. There is a private garden where herbs and special flowers are grown. A picnic shelter is at one end, and people can bring their food and eat there. Benches are located throughout the large complex where one can sit and luxuriate in the gorgeous weather.

Several bushes are entwined over and under each other in several spots where squirrels and rabbits hide under the shading branches. Beautiful trees are growing throughout the grass, and it is a paradise. I am grateful for the daily reminder of God's beautiful creations.

When we first discovered the huge spaces to run and play, I kept Sita on leash. Gradually, I gave my friend more freedom. I learned I could trust her. I would drop the leash and allow her to roam, and she would return. She chased the critters, never hurting them. She enjoyed the chase and would come back with a wide grin, satisfied she was the reason they all ran.

I learned early on how smart Sita was, and she trained me. When she started to veer off the playground into someone's yard, I would clap for her to come and give her a treat. After a couple of times, she learned the boundaries. However, she would go to the end of the playground, turn and look at me. I would clap, and she would run over. Then I realized she was doing this on purpose just to get a treat! Who was training who?

After a couple of times going to the special paradise to run and sniff, she had it all figured out. We would come home from work, and she would start jumping up and down at the door. She would pull me all the way to the wonderful fields and smells.

Together we watched the seasons change along with our romps in the weather. We plunged through the snowdrifts in the winter. We laughed and got wet in the rain. We took water bottles and stopped every few minutes when it was unbearably hot and humid. And we relished those spring and fall days when the air is neither too hot nor cold.

After an exhausting day at work, she still would run with the wind blowing back her ears and sniffing the breeze while I gazed at the stars and moon. I even bought her a blinking leash, so I could run her later at night since I would often work until 8 or 9 PM. It was our own little paradise together. But something unexpected happened to change everything.

The heavens declare the glory of God; the skies
proclaim the work of His hands.

PSALMS 19: 1

❧

Dear God,

Thank You for leading me back to the beauty of nature again and Your glorious works.

Amen.

❧

DEVOTIONAL NINETEEN:

Sita Finds a Friend

*A friend loves at all times, and a brother is
born for a time of adversity.*

Proverbs 17:17

One beautiful day Sita and I were on the playground. Several people were walking their dogs. We could not resist letting the dogs run freely as they sniffed and enjoyed themselves.

A gorgeous black Lab approached us running at full speed. Sita and I watched him. He suddenly stopped. He and Sita sniffed each other and began to run side by side. I talked briefly to his owners and discovered his name was Max. He had the shiniest coat I had ever seen. His brown eyes danced with merriment, and his features were perfect. His tail arched upward like a shepherd's crook. He looked like a dog out of a picture book. Sita usually became bored with other dogs, but this canine fascinated her. She wanted to play, and he complied.

Several days later, I was with Sita on the playground with a friend, who gasped as a large bundle of black descended on us. I laughed and explained this was Max. The daughter of the family accompanied him this time, and we talked some more. The dogs were having a wonderful time smelling every plant and blade of grass in sight.

I told Max's family that I taught at a community college and what my first name was. This is where the story becomes serendipitous. It was a busy first day of classes for the semester, and I entered the office where my mailbox was. The secretary handed me a note from Max's parents asking me to call them.

I contacted them and found out the entire story. Ken and Nancy are retired teachers, and we have a lot in common. They came to the community college the very first day of classes and entered the student center. When they told the receptionist they wanted Jane with a hearing-ear dog, she knew it was Sita and me. She directed them to the Psychology Department where my secretary got the note and gave it to me.

There was a reason they wanted to talk to me. They had taken Max to a heated indoor swimming pool, but he was afraid of the ramp leading into the water. The workers suggested he have another dog with him. Would Sita and I be interested?

We did take the dogs swimming at Healing Waters, and the partnership of a second dog for Max worked. Max was all boy and bravado and couldn't allow a girl dog to show him up. Sita went right in, and Max began to jump over her! Sita paddled around, and Max splashed and swam! The dogs bonded even more, but what was more amazing was that in God's gift of Sita, He also gave me the gift of great new friends.

We continued to meet on the playground through the next several seasons. The dogs loved it so much that Sita would bark all the way there. They jumped in the snowdrifts, splashed through the puddles, and chased each other up and down the hills. One picture of them jumping in the snow appeared in a calendar for Circle Tail. People thought it was Photoshopped and couldn't believe Sita could jump that high, but she did with Max!

Even people who didn't know us would walk by and comment on the special connection between these two Labs, one so light and the other so dark.

What was even funnier was that Max typically didn't like other dogs. When Ken and Nancy first saw Max bolt for Sita they were frightened. They were sure he would hurt Sita, but instead, the two dogs started had walking side by side and playing together. They were amazed at this special connection and a great friendship was formed between "the lady and the tramp!"

Be completely humble and gentle: be patient,
bearing with one another in love.

EPHESIANS 4: 2

❧

Dear God,

**Thank You for finding Max and his wonderful
family for Sita and me. We are so grateful for our
new forever friends.**

Amen.

❧

DEVOTIONAL TWENTY:

THE LADY AND THE TRAMP

No temptation has overtaken you except what is common to mankind.

1 CORINTHIANS 10: 13

People always laugh about Sita's "halo." She tries to be perfect. On the rare occasion she is not, she ducks her head and gives me that hangdog look. It breaks my heart when I have to correct her.

Even her friend Max is aware of the "halo effect." Max is a mischievous, gorgeous, black Lab who is truly sensitive, warm, and great with kids. He has a playful spirit and just loves life. Whenever Max is in trouble and is corrected, Sita still hangs her head, drops her tail, and looks upset that her friend is being disciplined.

Once when I was not watching, Sita ran across the road to chase a squirrel. I was scared to death that she would get hit and started yelling, "No! No! No! Never do that!" Sita was properly chastised and gave me that, "Oh no, I am a bad dog," look. I then petted her, letting her know that she was forgiven.

Max's family burst out laughing. I did not think this was funny and abruptly turned to look at them. Max was jumping up and down. He was thrilled that Sita was the one in trouble and not him. We all cracked up because that is Max.

One evening I was at Max's family's home for several hours to watch a baseball game. We went to get a pizza. The dogs were in the back seat. I keep dog treats in my holder for Sita, and she never touches them. Max, however, climbed from the back seat over to the front seat with his guardian and me both sitting there and stole Sita's snacks! When we returned home, Max managed to eat the cupcake holder that my cake was in. He ate off my plate of pizza and slapped Sita repeatedly to get her to play. Sita just shook her head and watched him. Somehow she instinctively knew she is a working dog even out of vest and that she should not act like Max.

I did not realize the influence Max had on her until he came to my apartment one day. Cesar's cat food is kept in the laundry room, while Sita is fed in the kitchen. The cat and dog are respectful of each other, and I can even feed them both treats at the same time, giving one a treat on one side of the kitchen and the other on the opposite side. That was until Max came. He found Cesar's dish and gobbled up all of Cesar's food. After he left, I refilled Cesar's dish, and Sita decided she would eat the cat's forbidden food. I sternly told her, "No," and she stayed away until Max's family came over without him a few days later. They started laughing at Sita, who was behind me. I turned around to see that she had dragged Cesar's dish out of the laundry room to the bedroom and was eating. The mere sight of Max's caregivers had triggered her to eat the food she was not supposed to.

We always assumed that Sita would be a good influence on him, but that never happened. It was the opposite! Forbidden fruits and temptation are around us daily. God knew how easily we are tempted when he gave us the Lord's Prayer.

And lead us not into temptation.

MATTHEW 6: 13

Dear God,

It is so easy to be tempted. It seems everywhere we look we see people and even animals pushing the boundaries of what is acceptable. Thank You, Lord, that you have set boundaries for us to abide by.

Amen.

DEVOTIONAL TWENTY-ONE:

No, She Is Not Perfect

No one should seek their own good,
but the good of others.

1 Corinthians 10: 24

There are people who say dogs can't talk. Maybe Sita doesn't use the English language like a human, but she certainly can communicate.

My veterinarian told me that Labs and retrievers make such good service dogs because they are treat driven. That is certainly the case with my beautiful dog. She will do ANYTHING for a treat!

Sita has been trained to pick up anything that I drop. This comes in very handy for a hard-of-hearing or deaf person. We are unable to hear if our keys slip out of our pocket or money drops to the floor. I may be walking along, and suddenly Sita gives a little hop, dives down, and emerges with my keychain dangling from her mouth. She throws her head up in pride and chomps happily on the treat I give her as a reward.

I have many allergies and constantly keep a pack of tissues in my pocket. If a pack or a single tissue falls, Sita performs her task.

However, she sometimes goes one more step. When my back is turned, she will go to the nearest wastepaper basket, pick a tissue out of it, and bring it to me. I turn and tell her, "You're busted!"

She strikes a pose of innocence. "Who me?"

She also has definite methods of making her wishes known. I was lecturing to my students in class on the serious subject of psychology. A peal of laughter erupted from the students. They were gazing at my dog. Sita was sitting behind me, slyly watching with her leash hanging from her mouth. Clearly, she was tired of my talking and was ready to leave!

Sita sleeps a lot like most dogs. When she is home, she doesn't want to play or interact with anyone. There are times the phone rings, and she doesn't bother to get up. When I am able to hear the amplified phone I will say, "Sita, let me know."

She answers with a bored yawn like, "You heard it. What do you need me for?"

Sita can be in her bed, allegedly dead to the world and appearing to be passed out. When I open the refrigerator door for a drink of milk, she is nowhere to be found. However, when I open the cheese bin, a large yellow Lab bounds into the kitchen with a wagging tail, begging for some of her favorite treats.

My first cat that I had paid all the medical bills for passed away two months after I got Sita. I was heartbroken and returned from the veterinarian very upset. Sita stood stoically as I came home and sobbed into her fur. She was a huge comfort to me.

I was not going to get another cat until a friend found a rescue cat that had lived in a dumpster for nine months before I took him. So I was without a cat for exactly two months!

I named my second cat Cesar, and it was an apt name. He took over my house immediately. He jumped on Sita and would try to play, intimidating her. Soon, the two of them had a truce where they were never friends but co-existed in the same house.

Sita is a lady and very well-trained. She will not bother Cesar while he is eating any of his food. But it is a different story if he drops or leaves behind any morsel of tuna or a treat. As soon as Cesar is out of sight, Sita gobbles down the abandoned edible.

She constantly keeps me on my toes, and I love her for it.

Sometimes we think we can get away with things with God. God knows we do these things and that we are not perfect. But He loves us anyway, just like I love my dog!

Above all, love each other deeply because love covers over a multitude of sins.

1 PETER 4:8

❧

Dear God,

Thank You for accepting us with all our imperfections. We are blessed by Your grace, and grace alone will save us from ourselves.

Amen.

❧

DEVOTIONAL TWENTY-TWO:

PUSHING THE LIMITS

May He strengthen your hearts so that you may
be blameless and holy in the presence of our God
and Father.

1 THESSALONIANS 3: 13

Sita is observant. She wants to be part of the action no matter where we are. If we are in a restaurant, she refuses to be placed in a corner. She insists on lying between me and the aisle. This makes sense because how else can she alert me? However, she can take this to an extreme.

I will be involved in a conversation with friends or family while eating. Then, I'll look over and find Sita smack in the middle of the aisle, several feet from where I placed her. She's moved the blanket out to where she wants to sit. This is often where she might trip someone. When I correct her, she gives me that innocent look like, "Mom, I am in place." Another trick she plays is to just have one toenail on the blanket. She gazes at me as if to say, "This works, doesn't it?"

Most of us tend to underestimate how intelligent dogs really are. When I was in graduate school, I had a friend I studied with who was blind. She had a beautiful Lab named Heidi. When I went to my friend's house to study, Heidi would be out of vest, and I could pet her. However, when we were in class, and Heidi was in vest, she would be corrected by her companion if she reached out to me for a pat on the head. Heidi knew the only way my friend would know she was reaching for a pat was if my friend felt the strain on the leash. She'd reach out with her nose just far enough to touch me but not pull. My friend never knew she did this to me, and I did not have the heart to rat Heidi out.

Sita has figured out that she could utter a tiny bark at an exact pitch that I am unable to hear. The only way I would know is if someone tells me. One of the most memorable times was while I taught a class. We had experienced a very long winter in Ohio. A gorgeous spring day had finally arrived, and everyone wanted to be outside, including Sita. She jumped up to alert me to a sound in the hallway and was reluctant to settle down again.

I told the students, "She is ready to play with Max after class."

I continued to lecture when I observed a look of astonishment cross the faces of my students. I asked what was wrong. They informed me that when I said Max's name, Sita uttered a low bark that they'd heard but I hadn't.

I gazed down and said, "Sita," in a disapproving tone of voice. Sita sank down with her head lowered and gave me a sad look. She really does want to please me and knew she was in trouble. I decided from then on to spell Max's name. (I wonder how long it will take my precocious dog to figure that out.)

Another trick Sita has is when we go out to eat. If I drop my napkin, she will retrieve it for a treat. Several times she has gone and whisked the napkin off my dinner companion's lap, then brought the napkin to me acting like he or she dropped it. The first time she did it, I was fooled until my mother informed me that it was her napkin. Now I have to be careful to check that the item was dropped and not stolen. Sita's desire overrides what she knows is wrong.

Sita truly wants to be a good dog and to please me, but sometimes it is just too hard for her. Then I do need to gently correct her. God does the same thing with us. We try to follow all God's laws but just cannot always do it. He is gentle with his corrections and loves us anyway. It requires a conscience to help direct our paths. I thank God for His gift of love and laws.

Make every effort to be found spotless, blameless, and at peace with Him.

2 Peter 3: 13

Dear God,

Why is it our tendency to be almost good? Help me to not push Your limits but to strive to live a life holy and blameless.

Amen.

DEVOTIONAL TWENTY-THREE:
BEING ABANDONED AGAIN

We belong to the Lord.

ROMANS 15: 8

There is a lot of debate around how much dogs remember from their past. Some dog behaviorists say they do not remember anything and only live in the present. They have no sense of time and greet their partner as enthusiastically if he or she has been gone an hour or a week.

Others dispute this and point out stories about dogs trekking miles when moved, only to return to their previous home. And many dogs seem to know when their owners are coming home from work.

Circle Tail's philosophy is in the middle ground. Marlys believed it would take Sita about six months to figure out her forever home was with me. She claimed that the dogs do not think about their past.

One of the drawbacks of training a service dog is that they are constantly switched from prison to foster home. The prisoners perform the basic obedience skills: sit, heel, lie down, and to obey, working on more than fifty commands. The foster parents train the dog in their vest. They take them to restaurants and public places, teaching the dog to settle, not to beg, and to follow basic commands.

Marlys said the dogs were switched back and forth so they wouldn't get overly attached to one person. She mentioned that different breeds reacted in different ways to the moves. "German shepherds tend to become very protective with one owner, while Labs are loyal to whoever is feeding them."

Sita and I bonded so beautifully that I didn't think about her abandonment on the streets and her past history. Marlys mentioned to me that she wished all the canine and human partners would bond as quickly as Sita and I did. However, I was reminded about Sita's insecurities by an unusual incident.

Tracy, Sita's foster mother, had several dogs and cats of her own when Sita settled into their home. Tracy was an advocate for Sita during a rocky time in the training program. When Sita returned from the first prisoner handler, she was shy and jumpy. It was debated whether she should be put up for adoption or go on to be a working dog. Tracy suggested a different trainer, and Sita blossomed. I'm grateful to Tracy for insisting Sita be a service dog.

Tracy and Marlys came to my home two months after I received Sita to assist me with training. When they finished, we left to drive and meet with two other people from Circle Tail who had service dogs. They lived in Cleveland about an hour away. It was decided we would all eat together at a local restaurant near the other people.

I gave Sita the command to get into my car. To my utter surprise, she began whining. These dogs are trained not to whine. I kept asking her what was wrong. I checked to see if she had to go to the bathroom and gave her some treats. Sita stopped whining but refused to settle down. Tracy asked what was wrong. I told her and she said, "Tell her to stop." Tracy came from the mindset of a trainer, so Sita was not allowed to whine under any circumstances.

"Tracy, she never does this, and something is wrong," I said.

Tracy walked off, and Sita did stop whining once we were in the car. We drove on up to our meeting place, and Sita and I followed Marlys and Tracy to meet the other dog-and-human companions.

We were at a Denny's restaurant and were quite a sight with three trainers, three companions, and three service dogs all at one table. Sita behaved perfectly. When we left to go to our cars, Sita put her head down and followed Tracy with the saddest expression I'd ever seen on a dog. I suddenly realized what was bothering Sita.

"Sita," I said, "You are coming home with me!" I had been partnered with Sita for only two months. She thought she had to go home with Tracy.

Sita had lived with Tracy on and off for a year and turned to Tracy for the next command. "Go with Jane," directed Tracy. Sita jumped into my car and finally relaxed, sleeping the entire way home. I knew then that she wanted to be with me. She realized I was indeed her forever home.

Marlys was exactly right about the six-month time frame. After we'd been together for about that long, I drove with Sita to Circle Tail and saw Tracy there in the driveway. I worried what her reaction would be and if she thought I would leave her. Sita jumped out of the car, ran over to Tracy with a wagging tail, and came back to me again. She knew where her forever home was.

There are times we all feel abandoned. What a blessing to know God never will leave us.

God said, "Never will I leave you. Never will I forsake you."

HEBREWS 13: 5

Dear God,

Help me remember that You will never abandon us no matter what.

Amen.

DEVOTIONAL TWENTY-FOUR:

GUIDANCE

Listen my people and I will speak.

PSALM 50: 7

I had to undergo sixty hours of training before I received my precious Sita. I read several books and watched films from experts like Cesar Milan. Repeatedly, I was told to be the alpha dog and the leader of the pack. I desperately wanted to do all the right things with this beautiful creature entrusted to my care. I was determined to be in charge. However, Sita had other ideas!

When I first was partnered with Sita, I was a counselor for a variety of age groups, mostly children. The private practice I was in dealt with a lot of abused children living with foster parents. I was anxious how the counseling sessions would work for Sita.

On my first day having her at work, I was apprehensive and uncertain exactly what to do. I left Sita in the room where I met privately with my clients while I went to the office to pick up my charts. My supervisor approached me and asked, "Can I see the dog?" I obliged and a bond was formed immediately between Robin and Sita. She thought Sita was gorgeous, and Sita responded to her positively.

When my first client arrived, I placed Sita's blanket as far away from the door as possible. I felt like she would be out of the way and not startle people entering the room.

Sita looked at me and moved to the door. I gave her the command to return to the blanket. "Place." She stayed for a brief second and then moved to the door. She was not showing any attitude, just stubbornly refusing to stay where I commanded her.

After several attempts to have her obey me, it dawned on me. How could she alert or bump me when she was on the other side of the room? How could she tell me about knocks on the door or warn me about a fire alarm?

Her training to obey me was superseded by her instinct. She knew she had a job to do, and I was not allowing her to do that!

Sita repeated this pattern in restaurants and other establishments where I tried to place her in a corner in the back of the restaurant. She wanted to be in front of me where she could see and hear everything. Nothing would divert her from that.

I finally gave up on this whole idea of always being in charge and telling Sita where to lie down. I no longer used the blanket as place. I command her to settle, and she chooses where that is going to be. It is always a better spot for alerting me. As long as she is out of the way and not in danger of being stepped on, she is allowed to be where she wants to be.

If only we could do that in our relationship with God. No matter who tries to distract us, we must stay focused on His commands and what He wants us to do. Our ideas may not be the same as His. God knows best.

If you love me, you will obey what I command.
And I will ask the Father, and He will give you
another counselor to be with you forever- The Spirit
of Truth.

JOHN 14: 15

Dear God,

Help me to get out of Your way and allow You to direct my path. May I always take guidance from You.

Amen.

DEVOTIONAL TWENTY-FIVE:

SITA, MY THERAPY DOG

*Even though I walk through the darkest valley, I
will fear no evil, for You are with me; Your rod and
Your staff, they comfort me.*

PSALM 23: 4

Little did I realize when I received my beautiful dog that she would not
only make my life better but help so many other people. Her talents as
a therapy dog are amazing, and I witnessed this repeatedly.

Shortly after I received Sita, I got a devastating call from some parents.
They had just adopted a child who I'd had as a client for several years.
He was one of my favorite children. His foster father, the only father

he'd ever known, had died suddenly. His adoptive family was bringing him into my office to tell him.

What to say? What to do? I was saddened because I had become very fond of the foster father. I was supposed to be the counselor, but that never makes this job any easier.

What I did not realize was I now had Sita. After I told the grief-stricken young teen the terrible news, he grabbed Sita and cried into her fur for a very long time. She did exactly what he needed: nothing. She was there for him and that was all that was required. She stood stoically and let him hang on to her knowing instinctively what to do. The mother and I had tears in our eyes as I told her, "God gave me Sita just in time." She agreed.

The next time I realized what a treasure I had was with another client. She was sobbing into her hands and unable to speak as all the terrible things that had happened to her in her past overwhelmed her. Sita had been sitting quietly under my desk. To my amazement, Sita stood up, reached to pull a tissue out of the box, and trotted to the client, handing the tissue over with her mouth.

Sita had never been taught this task, but she had watched me hand tissues to clients who were crying so many times that she knew exactly what to do!

We both gazed at her in amazement. "Sita, you just made my day!" my client exclaimed.

I chuckled. "You should pay Sita, not me!"

One of the most amazing stories is about a young boy under three years old that was being counseled by the psychologist, who was the owner of the practice. He had suffered a great tragedy when he'd witnessed one parent murder the other one. He was afraid, uncertain, and traumatized for good reason.

The psychologist always had treats for Sita, and the little boy was leaving her office when Sita came bounding up. She outweighed him by many pounds, and he cringed because he was obviously frightened of this huge animal that was larger than him.

What did Sita do? She lay down and watched him. Just laid down – nothing else. She did not lick him or try to win him over. As he gazed at her sweet face, he realized she was not a danger to him and began to pet her. I did not witness this entire incident, but my supervisor was so amazed, she told me about it later. My sensitive Sita seemed to be an extension of God's love.

We need to be more sensitive to each other. I worry constantly about what to say when someone tells me their bad news. What I've learned to say is, "I am here for you." I do not need to lecture, or say everything is all right, or ramble on – just that I am here for you. Just like God is for us.

Be still and know that I am God.

PSALM 46: 10

Dear God,

Let me know that You are always there for me. Help me to be a comfort for others when they need me.

Amen.

DEVOTIONAL TWENTY-SIX:

SITA AND MY MOTHER

*For The Lord comforts His people and will have
compassion on His afflicted ones.*

ISAIAH 49: 13

I had been partnered with Sita for a year now. She was a therapy dog
where I was counseling, beloved by the students where I was teaching,
and my daily partner. I was working the equivalent of full-time; part-
time counseling and part-time teaching, and I was loving all of it. Life
was good.

We went almost every day to see my mother and took her out to eat.
This became a big part of Sita's life. Sita was a favorite with the staff at
the nursing home. I'd take her out of vest and let her visit. She'd dash
down the hallways with both staff and patients petting her. We were in
a nice routine, working and then going to see Mom at night.

But things were beginning to change. Mom got bronchitis and never
got over it. She made trip after trip to the emergency room. I never took
Sita with me because of all the alarms and bells, but friends stepped
in and helped me by keeping her. When Mom failed to improve, the
doctors told us she had blood clots in her lungs.

Mom finally confessed to me that she knew she could not hang on much
longer. She hated to leave me but was ready to give up. Thanksgiving
approached, and she got to see all the grandchildren.

One Thursday evening, I went to visit Mom, and she kept saying to me
again and again, "Sita will take care of you after I am gone." My mother
had the sharpest mind for a ninety-three-year-old I'd ever witnessed,

and chills ran down my spine. She knew the end was near, and she was trying to tell me.

I explained to her that on Friday night I would be hosting a party for my students from class and would not be visiting her. She understood that with sixty people in my house going to see her would be difficult. The party was a success, but my heart wasn't into it.

The next afternoon, I received a call from the nursing home that Mother had a stroke. They asked me if she should be transported to the hospital. In a panic, I said I needed to contact my siblings. The nurse gently explained the decision needed to be made in a four-hour window, meaning now. I yelled, "I cannot make that decision alone!"

"What would your mother want?" the nurse asked.

I replied, "She would not want to go to the hospital." She had told me she was ready to be free of her broken body. With Sita beside me, I went to the nursing home. I was apprehensive and scared. A nurse approached me in the hallway outside of Mom's room and said, "Your mom is conscious, but she's paralyzed on one side."

I entered the room and took her hand. Mom knew me but could only speak out of one side of her mouth. She asked what had happened.

"You had a stroke, Mom," I told her. "They asked if you wanted to go to the ER, and I said no."

Mom said wearily, "No, I don't want to go back to the ER." She had already been there four times in one month. It was obvious that my mother was going to pass away that night.

She knew Sita was with me. She stood stoically next to Mom's bed and leaned on me to comfort me. Mom nodded, watching us together. I believe Mom felt at peace knowing I wouldn't be alone. God knew that my mother and I both needed Sita with us, especially that night. His timing is always perfect.

May your unfailing love be my comfort.
PSALM 119: 76

❧

Dear God,

Thank You for the love of my mother. I also thank You for sending me Sita. She is a comfort and a constant reminder of Your love.

Amen.

❧

My Mother Is Gone

*Be merciful to me, Lord, for I am in distress; my
eyes grow weak with sorrow, my soul and body
with grief.*

PSALM 31: 9

IN MEMORY OF
KATHERINE BIEHL "MOM"
SITA & DR. JANE

My stomach lurched, and I thought I was going to throw up. My
mother was really dying.

The staff came and told me I should not be alone. I called a cousin who
said she would come, though it was a terrible, snowy, windy night.
I called my sister and brother and prepared them for the worst. My
sister said she would be in from out of state on the next plane.

Unfortunately, there had been no time to contact hospice and Mom
was in excruciating pain. My cousin came and stayed with me. As
my mother writhed in obvious agony, I begged the nurses for some
relief and morphine for her. They could only give what the doctor had
ordered over the phone, and the physician wasn't about to order more

powerful drugs. She wasn't there to see the shape my mother was in. The nurses could only follow their instructions and were helpless, too.

Mom was conscious the entire time and worried about me. "I don't want you seeing me like this."

I left the room after a particularly bad contortion. I was breathing hard and panicked because I was so upset with the fact we did not have hospice, and she was in such awful pain. "No one should have to go through this, especially my mother who did so much for so many people," I thought to myself.

I was panting in the hallway with Sita beside me when my cousin came and said, "You can still say goodbye."

I walked in and took her hand, saying, "Mom. Go be with Dad. Go in peace." She shuddered and breathed her last breath. I looked at the nurse and said, "She is gone."

The nurse nodded.

Then I sobbed and sobbed as I stood by my beloved mother. Sita remained staunchly by my side as I petted her. My cousin patted me on the shoulder. My mother, my confidante, and my best friend was gone.

The next day I was still in complete shock. I went to the nursing home to pick up my mother's things. The nurse from the night before approached me and said, "That dog knew. When you said your mom was gone the saddest expression came over Sita's face. You were watching your mother and did not see her. I went home that night and told my husband, that dog knew."

What happened a week later astounded me even more! My relatives had all returned to their homes. I went alone with Sita to clean out my mother's apartment. She still had the apartment in assisted living, since she'd only been in the nursing home part for a few weeks. Sita always bounded in as I would say, "Where's Grandma?" She would search my mother out, looking in whichever room she was; whether sleeping or watching television or sitting at her desk.

When I entered Mom's place this time, Sita refused to follow me. I called her several times. She would not obey my command, but she finally lay down across the doorway.

Suddenly, I realized why she wouldn't come into the apartment. She knew my mother was not there. However, she was going to protect me.

Sadly, I packed up my mother's things with Sita patiently watching me. She followed me to the car and came back each trip, resuming her spot in the doorway.

What a comfort she was being to me. She was there and helping me with every step I took. What a blessing to know I didn't walk alone. God and my beloved Sita were my comfort.

Blessed are those who mourn,
for they shall be comforted:
MATTHEW 5: 4

Dear God,

Thank You for Your comfort and love. Thank You also for this gorgeous and sensitive dog You sent me to help me through this terrible loss.

Amen.

DEVOTIONAL TWENTY-EIGHT:

SITA AND MY ILLNESS

The Lord sustains him on his sickbed; in his illness
you restore him to full health.

PSALM 41: 3

I was tired all the time. No, it was worse than that, I was exhausted. I had suffered tiredness from having anemia before, but nothing like this.

Depression, I told myself. I was upset about losing Mom. I was working two jobs and reliving the awful experience of her death. I also was the executor of her estate and responsible for distributing her belongings and money. I would get better after it was all over, I told myself. But the exhaustion would not go away.

I was on a routine visit to my family doctor when I mentioned this. He knew me well and immediately ordered blood tests. Yes, I was anemic, and he prescribed iron. I was to come back several months later. I then got a call from the doctor's office that the blood count was going the "wrong way," and I needed to see a specialist.

Now, I knew seeing an oncologist could mean cancer. But I was in true denial. I had been sick with a sinus infection for a long time and was convinced this was why my blood count went down. I took Sita with me and went to the doctor.

This particular doctor was not a sympathetic person, and I did not care for her but wasn't worried. After all, she would just find I had some infection, prescribe antibiotics, and I would never see her again. She decided to run some blood tests and asked me to return.

Sita was with me for all these visits. She made everyone in the large waiting room smile, and the staff loved her. I was more concerned with watching her behavior than anything else. I returned a week later, and the doctor told me everything was fine with the blood tests. Since they had taken eight vials of blood, I figured I had to be okay. I exclaimed, "That is good news!"

She then said, "But we need to find out why your blood count is so low. You need to have a bone marrow biopsy."

You would think alarm systems would be going off by now. I was a little worried, but still thought it was just infections. I had an immune disorder I was born with, and that was kicking up. I had the biopsy and then another follow-up visit.

The doctor told me I had something called Myelodysplastic Syndrome (MDS). She would have to wait until some of the tests came back to see what medicine worked. It started to sink in that I had a rare form of cancer. She prescribed shots for the anemia and would then decide what medicine I would be on.

I left the office in a daze. Sita was by my side, quiet and obedient. I never was so thankful for her presence. I have a doctorate and know how to do research. I perused several articles and read as much as I could. It sounded like this cancer was treatable with chemo. Concerned that I may not understand all the treatment options, I asked a dear friend to go with me when I went back to the doctor. The doctor also was from another country and had a very heavy accent, which is difficult for hard-of-hearing people like me to understand.

My friend and I were waiting in the examination room when the doctor walked in. The first words out of her mouth were, "The average lifespan of this disease is 104 months."

The room swam as my friend grabbed my hand. I replied, "But you caught the cancer early."

"Oh, this is not Stage One or Stage Two but a blood cancer," she continued. "But we may find new medicines."

I left the office with tears streaming down my face and my friend comforting me. I was going to be put on chemotherapy, and my life was about to change forever. The only thing I knew for certain was that God would walk this journey with me, and He'd given me family, friends, and my beloved Sita, ever faithful and watching over me.

A man of many companions may come to ruin but there is a friend who sticks closer than a brother.

PROVERBS 18: 24

Dear God,

Help me to realize nothing will happen to me that You are not aware of. You will always be there for me.

Amen.

DEVOTIONAL TWENTY-NINE:

BEING ILL

Come to me, all you are weary and burdened, and
I will give you rest.

MATTHEW 11:28

The next few months after receiving the diagnosis of MDS, or cancer of the bone marrow, were extremely difficult. The chemotherapy had to be carefully adjusted, I kept suffering upper respiratory infections from a lowered immune system, and the Procrit shots to boost my blood count made every bone ache.

Additionally, I was coping with the real prospect of a potentially serious and fatal illness. But the first thing I did was get another doctor. I had friends who recommended a fantastic woman. She was not, "gloom and doom" but rather, "We are being positive, and there are all kinds of other chemotherapy and blood transfusions we can do."

She suggested I visit a major medical research center, Case Western University Hospital. Here I encountered another doctor who knew all about MDS and even stated a bone marrow transplant would be possible if the chemo didn't work.

I did not realize the richness of my many friends. They surrounded me with love, food, and prayers. I realized that God was not leaving me alone to cope with this. Most of my family lives out of state, but friends, who had become my extended family, stepped in to help.

My siblings were very supportive. I received loving messages from them as well as occasional visits.

Edlyn, who I had known for over thirty years, accompanied me to all the doctor appointments. She is one of those rare people that one encounters in life and is an angel sent by God. She was with me when I received the Procrit shots to increase my blood cells and alleviate the severe anemia. She heard the prognosis of living 104 months. She witnessed firsthand my depression and my tough times. She accompanied me to all my doctor appointments to be my extra set of ears.

My other angel was Sita. This book is about Sita, not me, but since we are so intertwined, I need to explain something. Sita knew things were not the way they'd been before. I was taking naps in the daytime. She was there to witness the terrible side effects, like diarrhea and losing more of my hearing. She saw me burst into tears when the doctor told me I had only a few years to live. She has that wonderful sixth sense many dogs do. I leaned on her for my comfort. What I didn't realize was that I needed to be leaning more on God, friends, and family and less on her.

Do not let not your hearts be troubled. Trust in
God's trust, trust also in me.

JOHN 14: 1

🖊

Dear God,

Help me to know that You are always with me and that You send the people into my life I need every single day.

Amen.

🖊

Everything We Do Has a Consequence

*Fools give vent to their rage, but the wise
bring calm in the end.*

PROVERBS 29: 11

Life changes quickly. I was dealing with several blows all at once. I was still grieving my mother's death. Previously, I'd visited Mom every day. Now that time was empty and created a huge hole in my life.

I was on chemotherapy and would be for the rest of my life. Blood cancer does not allow for the patient to be off medication. With this kind of disease, the protocol is to just control the cancer. I knew life would never be the same again.

Intense career pressures were overwhelming me because I was working as a counselor with children and adults who had serious problems of sexual abuse, physical abuse, and foster problems. I also had a busy teaching job with tons of paper grading.

All the while, my loyal dog stood by me. She was my constant companion through my loss, my realization my health had changed, my painful treatments and doctor visits, and working with so many other people's pain.

I was totally wrapped up in my own problems and took Sita for granted. She was young and healthy. What I failed to realize was the toll all of this was taking on my sensitive and perceptive dog.

Sita and I were at a special event sponsoring working dogs. She charmed the audience as we did several programs where I demonstrated how she picked up items for me, bumped me when my cell phone rang, and alerted me when someone knocked on the door. We went back to our booth, and I was extremely proud of her.

Another dog belonging to a friend approached me. To my utter amazement, Sita snapped at the other dog. I was shaken and apologized profusely to my friend.

Several weeks later, I went with Sita to another friends' house. When their dog approached Sita, she again snapped. Several similar events worried me greatly. If Sita continued this behavior, I would have to give her up as a service dog. I was hysterical.

My friend Karia, who owned the first dog Sita had snapped at, was also an excellent dog trainer. She was the person Circle Tail had sent to do my home visit, and we'd become fast friends. Shortly after all these events happened, we drove to Circle Tail together. Sita was in the back seat as always, and I'd thought she was asleep. I was describing all these events to Karia with tears rolling down my cheeks. Suddenly, I felt a nudge. Sita had touched me. She knew something was wrong.

"She is picking up on all of your emotions," Karia told me gently. "She knows that you have been through so much and is trying to protect you. Look at her now. She knows you are upset. She does not know exactly why, but the more upset she sees you, the more she is reacting."

I realized then how all my emotions had affected Sita. She was protecting me the only way she knew how, snapping at any dog who approached me as a potential danger. I was ashamed of myself because I had been so wrapped up in my problems, I had not realized what I was doing to Sita.

Later, Marlys confirmed this for me. "I have to remind myself that if I get upset, my dogs will, too. If you calm down she will."

Once I calmed down, so did Sita. We deal with the death of loved ones, we become sick, and we all die sometime. I needed to relax and enjoy every single day. If I did, Sita would. As I became calmer, she stopped snapping at other dogs. Our life and relationship went back to where it had been before.

I always knew there was a consequence to every action. My emotions and reactions almost ruined a near perfect dog. And when I acted calm, peaceful, and content, I felt better, and my health (and blood counts) improved! Jesus tells us that "the body is a temple," and we need to treat it that way – both mentally and physically.

Do you not know that your body is the temple of the Holy Spirit who is in you, whom you have received from God? You are not your own; you were bought at a price. Therefore honor God with your body.

1 CORINTHIANS 6: 19

Dear God,

Let me be calm and peaceful and know You are there for me. And let me be aware of how my actions can influence others, even a beautiful dog.

Amen.

DEVOTIONAL THIRTY-ONE:
GOD HAS A PLAN FOR EVERYONE

Be still and know that I am God: I will be exalted
among the nations. I will be exalted in the earth.

PSALM 46: 10

One of the hardest ideas for me to grasp is just to be. To sit quietly and not try problem-solving, or helping someone, or thinking about the next chore I need to do, but just to be. To relax in the moment, whether it is daydreaming, reading a book at leisure, or watching *NCIS*. Sita has taught me so many times to just be, and the rest will happen.

My sister and I entered a restaurant/winery together that we had never visited. The person tending the bar was a young, energetic, beautiful woman, and she started to pet Sita with my permission. I could tell by the way she stroked Sita's ears and scratched her in all the right places that she had a real love for and knowledge about dogs.

She had many questions about Sita, which I willingly answered. I never tire of telling the incredible story about Sita's being abandoned in the streets, rescued from the shelter, and trained in the prison. I enjoy telling people what she does for me and demonstrating how she picks up items that I drop, bumps me when there is a noise, and alerts me to anyone standing near me. I explained about her training, how I received her, and the orientation I went through. The fascinated woman shared how excited she was to go home and look up the website for Circle Tail.

I have always felt it is my mission to educate people about service dogs like Sita. I explain about Circle Tail, various disabilities that dogs can assist with, and enthusiastically relate what Sita means to me. I never know what happens afterwards.

Sometimes when people ask me questions about Sita, I become impatient because I want to talk or eat in peace. This time, I had an instinct there was more to the story, but I didn't want to pry.

My sister and I left the restaurant chatting, exclaiming what a great place to eat it was and raving about the delicious dessert we'd had. I figured that was the end of the story. I felt good about educating another person. God had put us together, and He does this all the time, even when we are not paying attention.

Commit to the Lord whatever you do, and your
plans will succeed.

PROVERBS 16: 3

Dear God,

Let me always remember that You have a plan, not just for me but for everyone I meet.

Amen.

DEVOTIONAL THIRTY-TWO:

ANSWERED PRAYER

"For I know the plans I have for you," declares the
Lord, "plans to prosper you and not to harm you,
plans to give you hope and a future."

JEREMIAH 129: 11

A few days later, I returned to this same restaurant. The woman I had spent so much time talking with during our last visit greeted Sita and me by name. Her face shone as she petted and fussed over my special companion. We continued our conversation from the previous week.

I sensed that she wanted to say more, and my counselor training kicked in. I cocked my head, listening to her intently. My face must have registered the aspect of caring because she took a deep breath. "I want to share something personal with you. One of the reasons I have been so excited about Sita and Circle Tail is that I am going blind!" Of all the things I expected her to tell me, this was not it!

She continued bravely. "I already can't drive, and my fiancé takes me everywhere. The doctors don't know how progressive this disease is or whether I will lose all of my vision. I may or may not. I don't know. It could be tomorrow or years from now."

I felt a sick sensation in the pit of my stomach for what this woman was enduring. "When you answered all my questions so patiently, I began thinking about getting a dog, and I may need one someday."

I shook my head in amazement at God's work. There was no way this person could know that I had worked with the blind population for seven years as a rehabilitation counselor. I'd written my dissertation on people who had hearing and vision loss. I loved working with these two groups more than any other outreach work I have ever done.

I have learned in my old age that there is nothing we do -- no job we have, or person that we meet -- that doesn't prepare us for the future. I excitedly provided her with information on where to apply for services including guide dogs in our state.

And the story doesn't end there. Several weeks later, I had made reservations at that restaurant to eat with a friend. I asked about this young lady, and the staff told me she was on a later shift. We were ready to leave when she appeared for work. She ran over to us with a beaming face.

"My fiancé and I were watching a program on training dogs last night. He said he wants to train dogs for the blind because of me. And this never would have happened without meeting you and Sita."

Tears filled my eyes as I reflected that there are no coincidences in life. Was it chance I had dropped in to visit this eatery twenty miles away from where I live? I just happened to be passing and wanted to stop at this new place. My friends and family make frequent trips to Amish country, where the restaurant is located, but this was the first time we had ever stopped there. Was it coincidence that Sita's quiet demeanor immediately drew this person in need to her? And that I had worked for seven years with people who are blind?

I don't think so – God knows our plan long before we do.

Since God planned something better for us so that
only together with us would they be made perfect.

HEBREWS 11: 40

❧

Dear God,

Let me just be and know You are doing all the planning for me and everyone on earth.

Amen.

❧

DEVOTIONAL THIRTY-THREE:

ANTICIPATION

*Therefore I tell you, do not worry about your life,
what you will eat or drink: or about your body,
what you will wear.*

MATTHEW 6: 25

I was learning a lot about faith between the death of my mother and the diagnosis of my cancer. Surprisingly, the best teacher for me was Sita.

Humans spend their entire lives anticipating. I call it the "what ifs." What if we had more money? We just know our lives would improve. What if we meet the right person, our soul mate, and live happily ever after just like in the fairy tales? What if we get our dream job and life will be wonderful every single day we go to work? The negative side of the "what ifs" is a dangerous mindset to think about. What if it storms tomorrow, and I can't get to work? What if I become ill and unable to pay my bills? What if my boss fires me, and I have no income? What if, what if, what if....?

Sita anticipates in an entirely different way. She uses total faith. She has learned that my hearing aids make a squealing noise when I first put them in my ears in the morning. She stands next to me eagerly waiting to bump me (she starts salivating when I pick them up off the dresser) and is ready to receive that tasty kibble.

When I first open my eyes and climb out of bed, she is certain to get a belly rub and turns over on her back eagerly. After I get dressed, she anticipates that we will leave and go somewhere (where does not matter), so she brings her collar to me before I open the door. On the rare days we have a snowstorm and do not go out, she is puzzled but shrugs it off and goes back to bed!

She anticipates when I pick up the tuna can that she will get a treat. She anticipates in the afternoon that she will go to play with Max and stands by the door anxiously waiting.

And she does not pout. If we have a snowstorm, she gets more sleep. If we do not go and play with Max, well, that is life. If she doesn't get the expected treat, she will shrug it off and not ruminate about it.

The difference between Sita and humans is she does not worry or stew or carry on. She has complete faith that she will receive the treat or we will go outside. She knows that she will be taken care of and does not waste any time worrying. She anticipates the good and doesn't worry about the bad. I am the world's worst worrier, and she sets such a good example for me.

Why don't we do this with God? Instead of anticipating that He will make us rich or powerful or happy, we can live our lives in faith doing the little jobs every day.

These acts of kindness can be hugging a child, calling a sick friend, or lending an ear to someone in trouble. What would happen in this world if everyone did that and knew that all our needs would be met?

If something doesn't work out, we do not need to ponder why or ask, "Why me? If it doesn't work out something else will. Sometimes we just need to go to bed and get some extra sleep.

God tells us all the time not to worry, and repeatedly, He works things out. But as humans, we think we need more, or know better, or did something wrong. We fail to heed His constant reminders of demonstrating how things work out. We of little faith are not as smart as our dogs. Just look at the scripture.

He replied, "You of little faith, why are you so afraid?"

Matthew 8: 26

Dear God,

Please let me get those "what ifs" out of my mind and trust in You!

Amen.

DEVOTIONAL THIRTY-FOUR:
SITA TEACHES ME TO BE HUMBLE

Be completely humble and gentle: be patient,
bearing with one another in love.

EPHESIANS 4: 2

The most significant trait in Sita is her humbleness. She is a well-known, if not famous, dog. She has had her picture on two different wine bottles, including a red wine named for her from Santa Barbara, California. She has a website dedicated to her. She has been the star of programs both local and out of state.

Additionally, she has a picture book written about her and a whole host of articles. She has raised hundreds of dollars for Circle Tail through several programs and benefits. But all she really cares about is love, belly rubs, and, of course, treats!

Even more important than her fame is that she has been a solace to so many people. Children from my private practice have cried in her fur, and college students petted her during finals so they were less nervous. She was the companion animal who loved and supported me when my mother died and when I was diagnosed with cancer.

An employee at the cancer center told me that she looks at the patient list for days before Sita's (and my) appointment because Sita makes her smile. It does not matter where we go, whether it is a bank, restaurant, or local store, employees know her by name, and some even have treats for her. One local eatery cooks a piece of bacon when she comes, and the servers argue good-naturedly over who is going to feed her.

She is completely humble and not at all aware of the huge impact she has made on so many others. Her influence is a part of her just being Sita. She doesn't think she is special in any way. I honestly do not think she realizes other dogs do not go to the places that she does. When we go to a hotel and get upgraded, I joke that she's gone, "From the streets to the executive suites."

When Sita is visiting with other dogs, she becomes a dog and chases and plays and has a great time. And her canine friends don't know she is any different from them.

Christ talks throughout the Bible about being humble. Jesus was humble and went among the people although He was Christ the King. He became a man even knowing that He was Lord. He healed the sick and cared for the poor and the wounded, yet He washed the feet of His servants. His example is that of humbleness, and ours should be also.

The greatest among you will be your servant.
For whoever exalts himself will be humbled, and
whoever humbles himself will be exalted."
MATTHEW 23: 11-12

Dear Lord,

Let me be humble like Sita and know any gifts I have come from You.

Amen.

DEVOTIONAL THIRTY-FIVE:

NEVER GIVE UP!

Not only so, but we also glory in our sufferings, because we know that suffering produces perseverance.

ROMANS 5: 3

One trait that I have learned from having cancer is perseverance. After more than eight years of chemo and enduring terrible side effects and pain, I have often wanted to give up. I went from oral chemotherapy to excruciating shots in the stomach. The very medicine that was saving my life caused me to lose more of my hearing. There have been times that I have just wanted to lay down and die. But I try never to quit, and as a result, the precious chemotherapy has given me extra years and quality of life. I have learned a lot from Sita in small and simple ways.

Sita loves tuna and seems to be part cat. She especially enjoys licking out the can after I give her and Cesar a spoonful of tuna every evening. Of course, my cat is way too persnickety to ever eat out of a can; he leaves that up to the dog!

The difference between cats and dogs is striking. Cesar must be fed carefully in a clean dish. If any food is left over, or he doesn't like a certain flavor, he will leave it until I remove it and clean out the bowl. He will acquiesce to eating off a paper towel on the floor, but if the tuna is a day old, he puts up his pink nose in total disdain.

Sita does not care. Food is food. This is one of the reasons I can relate more to dogs than cats. Give me a chocolate candy anywhere, and I devour every luscious, last, delicate morsel!

Sita has developed the habit of licking out Cesar's tuna can after greedily slurping every last bit of her own. She picks up the can and hands it to me for a treat.

One morning, I was in a hurry to leave and started out the door. Sita followed me all the way to my SUV. She jumped in the back seat while I got in front and started my car. We drove to our destination, and I dressed her in her vest and leash. She jumped out, ready to trot beside me into the restaurant. My eyes glimpsed a foreign object in the back seat where Sita had been lying down. I reached over to find a tuna can.

Sita has a set routine. Every morning she goes down the steps with me and out the front door to go, "hurry." We then proceed to the back of my apartment where the SUV is parked in a covered garage. This unbelievable creature had carried the can all the way down the steps out to go to the bathroom and into the SUV. She finally gave up and dropped it in the back seat. All unbeknownst to me!

The last mile of a marathon is always the hardest. The last segment for a driver after a long trip seems to be the worst, and the driver begins to be sleepy. The last part of a doctoral program, which is writing the dissertation, is the hardest and the one most students fail to complete.

As I drove to work, I thought about Sita. She was determined to finish that task of delivering the tuna can and hopefully getting the reward of the anticipated kibble.

How many times does God say to us, "Keep going. Keep trying. I am with you." But we fail to listen. We can all take a lesson from Sita's determination to do her job.

"Be strong and courageous. Do not be afraid or terrified because of them, for the Lord Your God goes with you; he will never leave you nor forsake you."

DEUTERONOMY 31: 6

❧

Dear God,

Let me not give up but go the extra mile in everything I do. Whether it is for my family, my friends, or my work, I need to persevere to the end like Sita.

Amen.

❧

DEVOTIONAL THIRTY-SIX:

BE STILL AND KNOW I AM THERE

But when you pray, go into your room, close the door, and pray to your Father, who is unseen. Then your Father, who sees what is done in secret will reward you.

MATTHEW 6: 6

One of the most important times of the day for me is when I can be alone. I love to read my Bible in silence. I enjoy going on walks with Sita and take pleasure in nature. I am not afraid to be by myself. In this modern world of technology, where we constantly need to be connected through Twitter, e-mails, phones, texting, messaging, and computers, it is difficult to hear God speaking.

Sita is constantly busy and with me for long hours on the go. The major difference between Sita and me is she knows when to stop.

People are often surprised to find out that Sita also needs her alone time. When she comes home, she goes to her large bed and stays there the entire time. She refuses to join me on the couch, the ottoman, or anywhere except a few seconds in the kitchen when she gets fed. I keep water next to her bed, and there she stays. She needs that sleep and that downtime. I know that about her.

When I first got her, Marlys told me she is a low energy dog. She does not require a lot of exercise or constant entertainment. This doesn't mean she doesn't love to be outside, to go on runs in the schoolyard, or play with Max. She needs and relishes this time. But when she rests, she rests.

If someone knocks on the door, she is right there to let me know. Otherwise, she is off duty, and I realize this.

I am more like Sita than I want to admit. I love people and have many wonderful friends. But I also enjoy my private time alone to reenergize my batteries, so I am ready to go out and socialize all over again.

Jesus spent forty days in the wilderness. God tells us to be still and know Him.

Be still and know that I am God.

PSALM 46: 10

❧

Dear God,

Help me be still like Sita and know You are there.

Amen.

❧

DEVOTIONAL THIRTY-SEVEN:

Sita's Happiness

*Our mouths were filled with laugher,
our tongues with songs of joy.*

Psalm 126: 2

A plethora of books have been written on how to be happy. I maintain I have learned that from my dog!

I constantly get the comment from people asking, "Does her tail ever stop wagging?"

I laugh and say, "Maybe when she sleeps!"

She loves to go anywhere. When I ask her if she is ready, even on those rainy and snowy days I don't want to leave the house, her response is instantaneous. She leaps in the air and scoops her collar off the floor up in her mouth, bringing it to me with joy.

When I take her to the playground for a run, she hangs her gorgeous head out the window and barks loudly the entire way up the drive to the school. She jumps out and runs and sniffs and is in absolute ecstasy. If there is a squirrel or two to chase, that makes it even better. When she runs back to me with her ears flopping in the wind, she is panting with glee. She's thrilled to see me and get a treat. When she receives a bone she jumps in delight. Every morning and every night, I give her belly rubs, and her teeth part in a huge smile.

Watching her play with Max illustrates true contentment to me. After they run, bark, and play, she lies down on the cement in the driveway and sniffs the air as if she has never smelled it before.

When we play fetch with the ball, she leaps up, runs, and chases it. She picks it up joyfully and brings it back. She actually bounces and then drops it with a wide doggy smile.

When I tell her it is feeding time, she wags her tail and waits patiently for me to give her the bowl of food. That is when she is the happiest of all.

But she could be a very sad girl. She was abandoned in the streets, and no one wanted her. She was not adopted in the shelter. She was ready to be euthanized when the woman from there called Circle Tail and told them she would make a great service dog.

She was shy and scared at first. When I tell people now how backward she was, they look at me in amazement. But since she has been with me, she has been loved and adored. She has gone many places and done a multitude of things, and she knows she is working. She has a purpose for living.

I always have maintained that children and dogs flourish if they know they are loved. And Sita's needs are very simple. As long as she has food, water, trust, pats on the head, and knows she can go places and work, she is happy.

Sita doesn't ruminate over wrongs done to her. She doesn't worry about the past or think about the future. When she is concentrating on working, she does that well, but when she is at play, she plays hard.

I am envious of her ability to go to sleep. She can lie down and in minutes be out like a light.

It puts me to shame. I complain about the weather, the traffic, filling out paperwork, and all kinds of minor things. It is honestly just as easy to be happy as unhappy. The Bible tells us to sing and praise and enjoy life.

Why can't I relax and be like Sita? God wants us to be happy.

Therefore, do not worry about tomorrow, for tomorrow will worry about itself. Each day has enough troubles of its own.

MATTHEW 6: 34

🐾

Dear God,

Help me to always be carefree and happy like Sita.

Amen.

🐾

DEVOTIONAL THIRTY-EIGHT:

GODLIKE TRAITS

Turning your ear to wisdom and applying your heart to understanding.

PROVERBS 2: 2

Once I figured out I didn't need to read a lot of books on happiness and serving others but could just watch Sita, I learned many more wonderful acts of faith from her.

Sita has kept me from harm many times by her instincts. She sniffed the car next to me when someone was in there to warn me before it peeled out of the parking lot. She let me know when there was a construction crane dangling over us. She turns her head constantly if someone is following me. Sita knows not to sniff, or to run back and forth in the back of the car, or to bark. But she was warning me and following her instincts.

How often do I do the same thing with God? I can be very stubborn and have told people that sometimes God "slaps me on the side of the head." I am convinced I should go in one direction in my life, and He has a different plan. When I follow His direction, it is obvious He knows best. I need to listen instead of saying, "No." Sita is smart enough to realize when she needs to go in a different direction, and I should be, too!

Another Godlike trait Sita has is to listen. I think it is very sad that people in our society today are too busy to listen. We may nod and agree, but do we truly listen to what people say? When I was a counselor, it often struck me that people were paying me to listen, really listen, and to care.

One of the reasons dogs are so special is they do listen. They do not talk or interrupt! Often when I am in the car, Sita is gazing out the window or lying down and relaxing. However, if I turn around and say, "Sita," her demeanor immediately changes. She sits up and gazes at me and cocks her head. One ear is turned towards me, and her body is taut with anticipation. It does not matter whether I am telling her that we are going to play with Max or that we are stopping at the pharmacy for a bone, she is truly listening.

After Sita lies down on her bed at night and before I go into mine, we have a ritual. I kneel down and pray while stroking her in her favorite places; her belly, her chin, her face. Sometimes my prayers are silent. Other times I talk out loud trying to figure out how to solve a problem. She never judges, doesn't get bored, and won't leave without letting me finish. How many humans do this?

Another trait that Sita has learned is to communicate. Assistance dogs are supposed to learn tasks, not tricks. These dogs aren't circus performers. They have been trained to partner with a human who has a disability and help that person. One of the tasks Sita learned was to pick up her leash on command. Since she goes everywhere with me, this helps me out. When my arms are full of groceries, or I'm dragging a carry-on in the airport, I do not have to lean over to grab it.

Sita has learned to communicate with her leash. If she gets bored, she will pick it up without my command and sit in front of me. In doggy language, this means, "Let's go."

When she gets impatient while I am standing and talking to someone, she will sit quietly for a few minutes. Then, almost imperceptibly, she will walk around me once, twice, three times, wrapping her leash so my feet are caught, and I can't move. If I reproach her and tell her, "No,"

Sita sits for a few minutes. Then, once again, I feel the leash wrapping around my legs. She is ready to go!

After we return home, we usually go to play with Max, take a run in the apartment complex where I live, or drive to the school where she has the luxury of dashing all over the playground. I will often be going through my mail and returning e-mails when I get that funny feeling someone is watching me. I turn to see her standing by the door ready to go.

The only time she ever makes a sound is when I turn to go into the playground. Suddenly, I hear sharp barking and whining from the back seat. She is so happy she is going to her favorite spot and can't contain herself. As soon as she is out of the car, she is off and running and doesn't bark again.

If I have been in a restaurant too long for her liking, she will begin to get up and down and up and down. This is similar to a child being bored. I usually tell her sternly to settle, and she will for a while. Then she forgets and jumps up again.

And what really warms my heart is when she comes and puts her head in my lap. She just wants me to know she is there and loves me. We don't always need to talk to communicate.

People who I know with strong faith in God are content. They follow their instinct. They find pleasure in everyday miracles. They are not constantly searching for more things. They have learned to be happy that God is in charge.

But Godliness with contentment is great gain. For we brought nothing into the world, and we take nothing out of it. But if we have food and clothing, we will be content with that.

1 TIMOTHY 6: 6

❧

Dear God,

Please help me to look at Sita and learn from her. To be obedient, to listen, and above all, to be content with what I have!

Amen.

❧

DEVOTIONAL THIRTY-NINE:

SITA AND HER HEALING TOUCH

So they set out and went from village to village,
proclaiming the good news and healing people
everywhere.

LUKE 9: 6

I have been upset lately by severe illnesses and the deaths of several friends and relatives. Loved ones have passed on, and I attempt in my clumsy way to comfort the family. When I first hear the news, my instinctive reaction is, "What do I say? What do I do?"

We are hardwired to comfort another person, but many times we inadvertently say the wrong things. Examples may include: "This is God's will. S/he is in a better place," or "God needed an angel." These are not ideas that most people grieving a loved one want to hear because they are experiencing so much pain from the loss.

Touch is so important. We often do not think about it. We are wired to show compassion through touch. Hugs, a hand over ours, or the brush of a child's kiss on a cheek are just a few examples of showing our love.

Think about the significance of a minister, a priest, or a rabbi blessing us when they perform a "laying on of hands."

Doctors and nurses use comforting touch daily in their healing when we are sick and feeling lousy. Massage therapists and Reiki masters use touch in their work. Even physical therapists and occupational therapists use touch as part of their repertoire of healing.

The Bible contains story after story about Christ healing the blind, the sick, the maimed, and the ill with a simple touch. He knew the importance of our hands to connect with the miracle of healing and spiritual connection.

The touch of a pet can also be comforting when we are sad. Sita was born with the understanding of how important touch is. When someone is crying, she comes and lays her head on the person's lap. When I don't feel well, she will come and place her cold nose on my leg. If a child or adult is upset, she will lower her head to be petted. There are several scientific studies about the importance of animals in healing, and it is proven that people who have pets do live longer. This doesn't surprise anyone who has a pet.

I've watched her with the hurting children in my counseling practice. She would go to them and allow them to pet her. Somehow, she knew they were in pain. And she has comforted me so many times.

No one taught her this. Dogs have an innate sense of how important touch really is. Sometimes humans need to be taught this. Instead of talking when a friend or relative is upset, you may just need to pat them on the shoulder.

I keep repeating that dogs can be smarter than people. Sita woke up one day with terrible eye infections and allergies. I immediately gave her Benadryl, but that didn't help. I became increasingly concerned and ended up taking her to the veterinarian. She was placed on steroids. It was a miserable time for her.

Just like people who are on these powerful medications, she was always hungry, thirsty, hyper, and constantly urinating, and she did not understand why. My heart ached for her. I would pet her, comfort her, and try not to correct her for behavior she couldn't help. This was especially problematic because as a service dog I couldn't afford to allow her to misbehave.

What really touched my heart was Max. The first time he saw her after she became ill, he walked over, leaned down, and licked her hurting eyes. Sita put her face up and nudged him lovingly.

Tears welled in my eyes. A dog who talks dog language but had not one second of counseling training knew what to do. He simply licked the wounded part and was there for her. Humans can learn a lot from that gesture! Sita recovered quickly and was back to herself in a few weeks. I am certain that if she could talk, she would say Max's licking her and my belly rubs helped her heal.

And the whole multitude sought to touch Him, for power went out from Him and healed them all.

LUKE 6: 19

Dear God,

Help me to remember that touch is often more powerful than words.

Amen.

Bearing False Witness

*You shall not give false testimony
against your neighbor,*

EXODUS 20: 16

If you ask anyone who has a certified service dog, there is one type of person who causes problems for the rest of us. This is truly one of my pet peeves. (No pun intended). There are a number of people who buy vests online and try to pass their dog off as a service dog.

The typical dog that performs a service for a person with a disability has undergone at least a year or more of intense training. They have been carefully taught to help each companion individually for a certain disability. Circle Tail carefully chooses these special dogs out of a plethora of dogs. They must have the correct temperament, willingness to work, and intuitiveness to help the companion. The total cost for all the selection of these dogs, plus teaching them to assist a person with a disability, can be anywhere from twenty-to-sixty thousand dollars for guide dogs with the people who are blind!

The human partner also undergoes intense training and must work with the dog constantly to be sure no bad habits are formed.

Marlys told me from the beginning that if I allowed Sita to misbehave, I made it bad for all service animals. I did not understand originally what she meant, but I sure do now.

People often are watching Sita and me when I am not even aware of it. I have had many individuals approach me and ask where Sita was trained. They then comment on how well behaved she is. I jokingly tell them she doesn't want to go back to prison!

When I was visiting a friend in Florida, I was told I could not enter a restaurant because a service dog had once chewed up the carpet. My friend and I decided to eat outside. It was a gorgeous spring day where we were and snowing back in Ohio! Legally, I was allowed in the restaurant, but another dog ruined it for me.

When I flew with Sita to Las Vegas for a wedding, I noticed the flight attendants were leery when I brought her on the plane. Several hours later, they confessed to me that they'd had a dog the previous week who'd run up and down the aisle. The two attendants complimented me on Sita's good behavior. I told them that other dog had not been a real service dog but rather someone trying to fly the dog for free.

There is a local restaurant I frequented before I got Sita. After I received her, the servers were nervous until they saw how well behaved she was. They told me they'd once had a service dog who'd eaten off the other customers' plates. Again, I had to explain that a dog who behaved like that would never make it through basic training. I saw the dog they talked about once on the patio with Sita, and frankly, I was afraid of it.

The law says that one cannot ask for certification but can ask what the dog does. I am open to telling people that she is my ears and explain about her training. Sita, like any other dog (or child), can have her bad days where she roams too far from my side or becomes restless, but she is promptly corrected.

It is not all about Sita or me. I admit it is a huge burden and invasion of my privacy to be watched and judged, but that is the fact of the matter. If Sita behaves, she makes it so much easier for the next dog that wants to come into a restaurant, movie theater, or public place.

I am certain that people who try to pass their dogs off as service dogs think they are not hurting anyone, but they are. I feel strongly that it is the same thing as bearing false witness. Lying doesn't just hurt the person doing it. Others are also influenced and punished. Jesus addressed this issue in several Bible verses.

Therefore, each of you must put off falsehood and speak truthfully to his neighbor, for we are all members of one body.

EPHESIANS 4: 25

Dear God,

Let us all realize that if we tell any lies we truly do hurt others.

Amen.

DEVOTIONAL FORTY-ONE:

SITA AT CHURCH

*Then the man bowed down and
worshipped the Lord.*

GENESIS 22: 5

I decided I wanted to find a church closer to where I lived with a slightly different philosophy. I had belonged to my former congregation for a lifetime and was nervous about starting in a new place of worship.

I told my sister, "When I find a new church, they will have to accept Sita. Otherwise, I could not join." Legally, a service dog does not have to be permitted in any church because of the separation of church and state. However, a church could welcome her if the congregation wished. But it was more than that. I wanted them to accept her, not just tolerate her.

I tried a couple of churches before I found the perfect fit. We open every service with a mission statement. The minister begins, "No matter who you are or where you are on your journey..." The congregation responds, "I am welcome here."

Sita loves to come to church and jumps anxiously out of the car. When we go there, she is never in her vest, so she can be petted and adored. She enters and begins to greet everyone eagerly. Some churches I have attended have greeters at each door giving handshakes. In our church, people are truly happy to greet Sita.

When new members walk in, they are astounded to see a dog run up and welcome them. Her gentle manner wins her friends immediately.

Recently, a very dear and beloved member of the church passed away from cancer. Sita and I attended the memorial service. Her grandson asked me to sit with them because Sita made him feel better. Initially, I left Sita in the front row and sat several pews back because I was not family. She kept coming back to me. Finally, the husband of the woman who'd passed came and told me to join the family. His grandson needed Sita, and he knew that!

After Sita had surgery and was not able to come to church for several weeks, another teenaged young woman took up a collection of bones, treats, and toys from the congregation and gave Sita her own special basket when she finally returned!

Her own bowl with her name on it is there for her water. She follows me into the sanctuary and sits quietly at my feet during the service. If I read the liturgy or perform a song in sign language, Sita is by my side gazing.

The pastor told me that just watching her walk down the aisle gives one a sense of peace because she is such a peaceful soul. After all, dog is God spelled backwards!

Sita has also been a huge asset to the congregation. There have been parents who've come to me to tell me that their children were afraid of dogs before they met Sita. She instinctively seems to know to be gentle and approach a child cautiously. Sita and I have gained a lot from this church including love, acceptance, and spiritual guidance. But I need to emphasize what she has given.

This wonderful congregation has collected carloads of items for me to take to a local rescue center because of Sita. Sita is not just on the receiving end but the giving end as well.

As a result of Sita's influence, the church is pet-friendly, and she is a coveted member. And I am convinced God guided us here. I found out the previous pastor had a pet dog she brought to church. When Sita appeared, they were prepared for her. That couldn't have been a coincidence!

It is amazing what happens when a dog, people, and a church all get together!

"For where two or three come together in my name,
there am I with them."

MATTHEW 18: 20

❧

Dear God,

Thank You for helping me to find a church family with a wonderful congregation who loves both of us.

Amen.

❧

DEVOTIONAL FORTY-TWO:

GOD DOES ANSWER PRAYER

I will give you the keys of the kingdom of heaven.
MATTHEW 16: 19

The world as Sita and I know it suddenly became very dark. Our friend, Sharry, who'd taken care of Sita for me many times, was very ill. Wonderful, loving, caring, positive, spiritual Sharry was being overcome with a violent form of cancer.

I knew Sharry'd had surgery and was not doing well. When a text came in the middle of church, my stomach sank. Immediately after the service ended, I read the words from her daughter, "Mum is in hospice."

That could only mean one thing, Sharry was dying. I started to cry as Sita sat in front of me and kept putting her paw on my knee. She knew something was terribly wrong. The minister noticed and came over to me, concerned.

I debated what to do. Was this a time for the family to be alone with Sharry? Would she want me to see her sick? Should I just let it go, or should I offer to go to see her?

I prayed, and the answer came immediately. Sharry may want to see Sita. Because Sita was a service dog, she was allowed in the hospital and hospice.

I texted her daughter, Tressa. "I do not want to invade your privacy, but do you think your Mum would want to see Sita?"

The answer came, "I need to see Sita."

Sita and I drove to the hospital where Sharry was a patient. Tressa greeted me and guided me to Sharry's room. She was surrounded by loving friends and family. To my shock, she was totally unconscious, only being kept alive with a respirator.

Tressa explained that everyone was saying goodbye, and after the last rites, the tube would be pulled. A few more breaths would occur, and she would pass over.

Tressa motioned to Sita to jump on the bed. Sita did and lay down on Sharry's lap. There was no response, but Sita seemed to know that was where she belonged. We all stroked Sita and cried together.

Tressa then shared with me that her mother's last request had been to have a dog with her. Tressa had thought that there would be no way to arrange that. A few minutes later, my text had arrived. Yes, there would be a dog there and a dog Sharry loved like her own. Tressa is certain Sharry nodded and understood her when she whispered to her mum that Sita was coming. Sharry slipped into a coma and never regained consciousness.

Several of Sharry's friends and family, whom I knew, came to say their goodbyes. All of them pet Sita. Finally, the priest arrived, and it was time for us to leave. Sita did not want to jump down from the bed.

I stated, "Sita does not want to leave Sharry."

Someone answered, "None of us do."

With a sick feeling in the pit of my stomach, I was slowly realizing that I had lost a dear friend and a good human being. God had answered Sharry's prayer and allowed us to be a comfort for a wonderful friend.

*If you believe, you will receive whatever
you ask for in prayer.*

Matthew 21: 22

❧

Dear God,

**Help Sita and me through the tough time of losing
Sharry. Thank You for hearing Sharry's last request
and allowing Sita to be a minister of Your love.**

Amen

❧

DEVOTIONAL FORTY-THREE:

IF YOU PASS THIS WAY BUT ONCE

For we are co-workers in God's service; you are God's field, God's building.

1 CORINTHIANS 3: 9

It had been the perfect Thanksgiving. I had been with my sister and her family, whom I love and enjoy very much. We had eaten, visited, and shopped all weekend. I was flying back with Sita from St. Louis to Cleveland. The weather was beautiful, which added to how special the holiday was. Snow and rain can hold up passengers for hours in the airport.

Sita and I were at the gate and the first ones to board. We started down the tunnel, only to have an employee step in front of us and command us to turn back. I wasn't anxious yet since I figured they needed to get a wheelchair or help someone else.

The reservationist started making an announcement, and my heart sank. A part of the airplane was in need of repair, and all the passengers were being detained. My dismay increased as the delays became longer and longer, and many passengers were being rerouted to other flights.

My frustration grew because I couldn't hear the announcements nor could I speech read because the microphone was covering the gate agent's lips. I informed her that I could not hear, and she promised to keep me apprised of the situation.

A restaurant was located across from the gate. The agent graciously gave me a lunch voucher, and I told her where I would be. She kept announcing updates. She was swamped by swarming passengers but remained calm and focused.

I was reminded of the goodness of strangers. A gentleman behind me at the restaurant realized Sita was a hearing-ear dog, and each time an announcement was made, he told me what was happening. The airline reservationist came over to the restaurant to let me know about the progress being made. The replacement plane was being flown in from Newark, so it would take a long time.

The server in the restaurant realized our plight and allowed us to stay in the restaurant as long as we wished. The Ohio State vs. Michigan game was playing and several of the fans (including me) were faithfully cheering for Ohio State. After all, the plane was bound for Cleveland!

I was still anxious because it now appeared that we would be delayed for several hours. I told the other passengers that Sita would be in misery. This beautiful dog would never go to the bathroom inside but would hold it until she became ill. Legally, the airports are required to have a section where service dogs are allowed to go. This didn't always happen, though, because the laws had been so recently enacted.

The reservationist came over and offered to take Sita outside. She explained it would be difficult for me to take her back and forth through security. Fortunately, part of Sita's training involved her being able to go with someone else on my command. The reason for this training was just for emergencies such as this. Off she went with her tail wagging. The reservationist, who gave me her name, made me keep her badge in exchange for my dog! She obviously knew what this dog meant to me. I told her I trusted her, but she insisted.

They didn't return for some time, and I started getting concerned about Sita. A happy dog face and joyful bounce finally appeared. The employee apologized for taking so long. The airport made them go through security, and she was impressed with how well Sita followed her commands to stay and come. She shared that Sita had been totally focused on her.

Finding a place that was quiet without the noisy airplanes coming and going was difficult, but she'd found the right spot. That wonderful woman took Sita out twice during a seven-hour delay.

I got home late that night tired and worn out. But I pondered how wonderful the employees and other passengers had been. I felt a tinge of sadness that I would never see them again. They certainly made an impact on Sita and me. God tells we are here to help and serve others. In this busy world, we tend to forget. But in the St. Louis airport that day, several people followed God's Word.

Do to others as you would have them to do you.

LUKE 6: 31

❧

Dear God,

Let me offer to others the same comfort, kindness, and compassion shown to me. Let me remember to go out of my way to serve others.

Amen.

❧

DEVOTIONAL FORTY-FOUR:

Sita and the Children

Jesus said, "Let the little children come to me, and do not hinder them, for the kingdom of heaven belongs to such as these."

Matthew 19: 14

Sita and I have given many programs through the years, but there is one that especially touched my heart.

My sister asked me to fly to St. Louis and conduct two presentations to adults on Sita for her church. I also attended a craft fair, signed books in a wonderful little local bookstore, and happily visited with her and my brother in law.

We arrived at church, and Sita impressed everyone at the two appearances we gave. I sold several books and went back to Ohio, not realizing the impact Sita had made.

My sister sent me a note that the director of the church preschool had attended the event. Each year at Christmas time, the children do chores around their homes and bring the earnings to school. The money goes to a special charity. They had decided to make Circle Tail that year's project.

The three-to-five-year-old children came to school every day for several weeks with coins and bills in their hand for the doggies. They placed money in the jar and watched it grow.

Meanwhile, I had already decided to go to St. Louis for Christmas. It was arranged that I would attend the Christmas Eve service where the children and the teachers would present Sita and me with their donation.

I was so touched by the children's act of generosity. The teachers informed my sister there would not be a lot of money. However, the act of caring and sharing meant more to me than anything. Before the service, we gathered in the atrium.

The teachers presented me with a check for $277.69. My eyes filled with tears. This was truly what Christmas and giving was all about. These young preschoolers already had the experience of service and giving.

I must add a postscript to this story. I offered to conduct a special story hour and demonstration of what Sita did for the children. Sita and I returned the following May. The children loved the program and had finally met the real Sita. The teacher mentioned that it took them a while to realize that Sita was the same dog from the book, Here to Bump and Bump to Hear.

One little girl gave me a dollar that she had brought to the school too late the previous December. I had to swallow a lump in my throat as I accepted the dollar bill.

I happily sent the money to Circle Tail, and I am sure many dogs were fed and helped. I remembered Jesus teaching the apostles about the widow who gave all she had. These children had given everything they had earned.

Calling his disciples to him Jesus said, "I tell you the truth; this poor widow has put more in the treasury than all the others. They all gave out of their wealth; but she out of her poverty put everything – all she had to live on."

MARK 12: 43-44

❧

Dear God,

Help me to have the generosity of these preschoolers.

Amen

❧

DEVOTIONAL FORTY-FIVE:
SITA'S BAD WEEK

*But how can I bear your problems and your
burdens and your disputes all by myself?*

DEUTERONOMY 1: 12

We all have days, or weeks, where absolutely nothing goes right. What I didn't know was that dogs have bad days, too.

It all started when Sita was at a friend's house playing with two of her favorite playmates, a wolfhound named Liberty and a white German shepherd named Candy. I was crossing the lawn with her when a boxer came out of nowhere and attacked her. The nextdoor neighbor had not put on the collar for the invisible fence. The boxer was known to attack dogs and people.

My friend called the owner and demanded he claim the dog immediately. Sita wisely turned her head, lay down, and assumed the submissive position, which may have saved her life.

But her playmates were on her side. Liberty and Candy knew Sita was part of the pack. They swept in, barked at the aggressor, and chased the boxer until she disappeared. Poor Sita was shaking uncontrollably while I comforted her.

Sita seemed all right until that night she shot up in her bed trembling. I held her and made sure there were no wounds. I realized that she had been dreaming and was most likely revisiting the attack. I soothed and petted her until she fell asleep.

This was not the end of her bad week. Five days later, I was outside on the patio of a local restaurant. I was staying overnight at a hotel in preparation for a presentation on working dogs the next day. My friend, Karia, the master dog trainer, and I were enjoying the beautiful evening. Sita was seated beside us relishing the fresh air.

Several people had approached us asking about the dog and what tasks she performed. Before I could react, an inebriated six-foot man headed for Sita. I grabbed her protectively and said, "Please do not pet her, she is a service dog."

He was so intent on her, he totally ignored me. He came down on top of her and was ready to grab her in a bear hug. A prickly sensation started in my throat as I realized there was no time to rescue her.

Karia, was closest to him and came to the rescue. She grabbed both his wrists and demanded, "She is a service dog. Leave her alone!"

The man teetered backwards, and an astonished expression crossed his face. His brow furrowed and eyes narrowed.

Karia explained, "She is a hearing-ear dog and is working, so she is not to be touched." Obviously, the intruder had not bothered to read the sign on her vest that stated: "Do not pet." He apologized and moved on.

The next day, I was manning the booth at the convention for working dogs when a woman approached Sita and me with a terrier. To say the terrier was in a frivolous outfit is an understatement. A tutu was wrapped around his little stomach, and pink frills circled his face. He did not look happy.

The owner exhibited anxiousness, and I started to feel uneasy. She explained that her dog was a therapy dog. She started to ask me about dogs to help people relax.

I explained that there are psychiatric and trauma dogs, but they are highly trained. As she edged closer and asked why they needed to be trained, the hackles began rising on my back. I instinctively reached out to pull Sita back, but it was too late. The terrier bit Sita on the nose. Poor Sita jumped back in perplexity.

Again, I was upset. Again, I was concerned for Sita. My dog was being so good. The humans and other dogs were behaving badly. I sternly told the woman she shouldn't have a dog that bit others, that therapy and service dogs need to be trained, and her dog's actions were unacceptable.

Poor Sita had a doggone bad week! Thankfully, God gave her a calm and sweet disposition. She didn't dwell on her trying week but went on merrily, trusting tomorrow would be better. I could learn from her.

Do not let your hearts be troubled.

JOHN 14:1

Dear God,

Let me know that bad days and weeks are part of life and put them behind me as Sita does.

Amen.

DEVOTIONAL FORTY-SIX:
No Children

There are different kinds of service,
but the same Lord.

1 Corinthians 12:4

I have had a great life. My family and many friends have opened doors to travel and new adventures. I love my programming and writing. My apartment is cozy and inviting. I have a wonderful church and many friends who I go out with frequently.

I am involved with volunteer efforts for two separate animal rescues. Sita and I spend time in the community educating groups about service dogs.

I love to pursue my interests which include exercising, watching sports, writing, and reading.

For a long time, I had one huge regret. I didn't have children. I love kids, but through a variety of circumstances never bore or adopted any.

Sita has never been a mother, either. She was spayed as soon as she entered the program at Circle Tail. I have been asked by both children and adults why she was never a mother. I patiently tell the inquirers that service dogs are not permitted to have puppies because it distracts them from working.

Yet when I see her gentle nature, I think what a nurturing mother she would have been. One day it dawned on me...an epiphany. How Sita has touched countless lives through her programs, the clients I counseled, and the students in my classes who had met her. In our little town, servers know her by name and greet her, often slipping her a treat in addition to bringing her water. Even the people who dog sit for me say what an addition she is to their homes. When Sita was incapacitated and unable to go out with me for several weeks, complete strangers walked up to me at the Y where we exercised and at restaurants we frequented commenting that they had missed my beautiful dog!

Sita's destiny was to mother many people. I realize now that I, too, have had the opportunity to influence many children through my service as a librarian, a counselor, a teacher, and a writer. I had time to work with far more children because I didn't have my own. My mother often told me that I did not have children so I could influence others for the better.

God has plans for each and every one of us, human and canine. I accepted that He had a different plan than I did and that I was blessed.

Commit to the Lord whatever you do and your
plans will succeed.
PROVERBS 16:3

Dear God,

Thank You for Your plan for
my full and happy life.

Amen.

DEVOTIONAL FORTY-SEVEN:

Let the Good Times Roll...

He will yet fill your mouth with laughter and your
lips with shouts of joy.

JOB 8:21

Sita and I have shared many great times together, and there are so many wonderful and funny stories. I regale my friends and family with each new adventure we have.

I have patiently explained to people she is a hearing-ear dog, and the response several times has been, "Oh, so the dog is deaf?" I then have to tell them that it is not the dog who is deaf, but me. This puzzles some people until they see her bumping me and what she does to assist me.

I chuckle about the time I went to a Denny's and was brought a Braille menu. I thanked the server because his heart was in the right place. I recall with humor the time Sita and I stopped at a McDonalds. An elderly couple was in the next car watching me intently as I got out of the car and put Sita in her vest. We walked into the restaurant, bought our food, and came out. I became uncomfortable because they were still in their car staring impolitely at me.

Finally, the woman got out and approached me. "We have been watching, and we wondered if you are blind? If you are, how did you drive in here?"

I remember fondly the time we were eating outside, and two elderly women were next to us staring. One of them eventually asked, "What would your dog do if I touched you?" I explained hastily she was not a guard dog, but I am not sure the women believed me as they appeared frightened of her.

One of the most hilarious times was when a woman approached us in a restaurant with so much makeup on it was caked. Sita was lying quietly on the floor next to me. The customer started to lean over and make kissing noises.

I grabbed Sita and said," She is a working dog. That is why there is a sign on her vest that says, do not pet."

The woman replied, "Oh, I am not petting her. I just want her to lick me!"

It has been said that people are the only creatures on earth that have a sense of humor. I am not sure I believe this because I watch Sita smile when she is getting belly rubs. I also firmly believe that God allows us to laugh, so we can endure the hard times. Nothing helps me through a bad time more than humor and a good chuckle.

I do know that this wonderful canine and I have been through so much together, and she makes me laugh all the time. She has been a gift from God who wants us to be happy and shout with joy.

He will yet fill your mouth with laughter and your
lips with shouts of joy.

Job 8:21

❧

Dear God,

Thank You for teaching me to laugh and for the great times Sita and I have together every day!

Amen.

❧

DEVOTIONAL FORTY-EIGHT:

GOOD DEEDS

*If it is to encourage, then give encouragement: if it
is giving, then give generously.*

ROMANS 12:8

There are many negative stories about service dogs, and I read about this all the time. But then there are the positive stories.

After many years with Sita, I can share both good and bad. On this particular day, I was feeling especially jaded because a local restaurant Sita and I had frequented for many years had asked me for papers and hassled me. This is illegal. I was most upset because the comment made by the employee was, "We have seen you here before."

They let us enter, but when I later read reviews on the restaurant, I discovered that another service dog had been turned away as well. When I posted my comment that this was against the ADA, the website removed my post!

I was ruminating about this while Sita and I were wandering through the dog treats aisle at a local grocery looking for a special bone that Sita likes. An older woman approached me and asked about Sita. I didn't stop to talk but answered her questions politely about what kind of service dog she was as I scanned the aisle.

"I found the bones," I said, waving them in the air because I was happy!

Her next action totally blew me away. She reached into her wallet and handed me a ten dollar bill. "I want to pay for them."

I stopped abruptly and faced her in surprise. "You don't have to do that, but thank you so much!"

I started to return the money, but as I looked into her sweet face with the smile, I changed my mind.

"I want you to keep it," she said softly.

I accepted the money and told her, "I will give it as a donation to Circle Tail." I started to explain more about the program, but she turned away.

I dug in my purse for my card describing the website on Sita. She came back to talk to me some more. "Oh, I thought you were giving her a treat!" she exclaimed. This kind woman was not interested in any more inspiration but simply wanted to do something sincere for my dog. I thanked her profusely, and we both resumed our shopping.

I left the store feeling wonderful. This woman had timed it perfectly. She gave me more than money that day; she restored my faith in humankind. God wants us to be good to one another and make people feel happy, not sad. This woman had no way of knowing how happy she made me with this well-timed and generous act. But God knew.

Each man should give what he has decided in his
heart to give, not reluctantly or under compulsion,
for God loves a cheerful giver.

2 Corinthians: - 9:7

Dear God,

Thank You for the people like this woman who wanted to do something for Sita and wanted no fame or credit but simply wanted to give. May I be more like her!

Amen.

DEVOTIONAL FORTY-NINE:

JOY

Weeping may stay for the night, but rejoicing comes in the morning.

PSALM 30:5

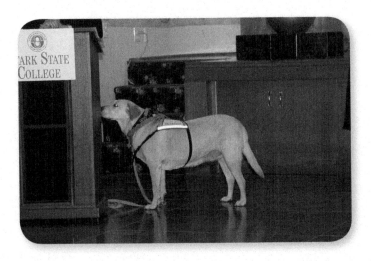

Dogs are amazing when they express joy, and Sita is no exception. She had a rough beginning and initially was insecure. After she had been with me for a while, she became the most jubilant dog around.

If I am waiting for someone to pick me up in their car, I will say, "Sita, let's go see." She races down the stairs, rushes out the door, and greets my friends at their vehicle. If it is someone she knows well, she jumps in glee because she is happy to see them!

If I am gone, even for a short time, when I return, she bounces up and down because she is so excited that I'm back. I keep saying I wish everyone was as happy to see me as my dog!

When we go to restaurants, I often save a piece of food to give her outside. The patrons are amazed when this quiet, well-behaved dog races out the door and jumps up in delight at getting her treat! A simple little sample, and she acts like I gave her a fortune.

One of my favorite stories is when I was at the dentist. I was flat on my back and could not see her. She knew I could not hear her. She usually just lays down next to me and often puts her head on my dentist's foot. He loves her just like the entire staff.

This visit, he doubled over laughing.

"What?" I asked.

He said, "She knows you can't see or hear her, and she slipped out. Sita pranced down the hall to visit every single patient."

I apologized. He explained they all loved her. She came back by the time he was done with the treatment and looked at me with an air of innocence. If not for him, I never would have known she was gone.

Some banks, restaurants, and doctor's offices keep bones for her. She trots in proudly, and then when the server or the staff person or the teller acknowledges her, she begins to show off. She'll stand on her hind legs, shake their hand, or do anything for a little treat.

Four years after I got Sita, I received an award that meant so much to me. I was selected for the Excellence in Faculty award at the community college where I taught. I missed my parents desperately because they would have been so proud. But Sita accompanied me, and there are several pictures of her gazing at me with her loving eyes as I accepted the plaque. She stole the show as usual!

And for Sita, it is all pure unadulterated joy. She does not need or want expensive toys or sirloin steaks. A little kibble, a pat on the head from a person she knows or doesn't know, or just some praise makes her a happy dog.

We can learn from this. God wants us to be joy-filled, too. And it does not have to be a new car, house, or lots of money. It can be the sunshine, a cup of coffee, or talking with family and friends. It can be a child's laughter or the companionship of a good dog.

This is the day the Lord has made; let us rejoice
and be glad in it.

Psalm 118:24

Dear God,

Let me be joyful and happy with life and all the wonderful things You have created. Every day is a new beginning.

Amen.

DEVOTIONAL FIFTY:

FULL CIRCLE

I have now been partnered with Sita for more than ten years. It is hard to believe that it has been that long. Many changes have occurred for both of us. My cancer forced me to leave both my counseling and teaching jobs, and now I do freelance writing. We have moved to a smaller apartment that I am more able to take care of.

Sita has slowed down a lot. Recently, she had a surgery for arthritis of the elbow. She had been limping for several months and was in terrible pain. Once the arthritis was cleared out, her limp improved. Unfortunately, we had to be separated for several weeks because she was unable to handle the steps to my second-floor place. The veterinarian and staff stepped in and took care of her along with my friend Edlyn and her family.

This was a horrible time for both of us because we had to be apart, and Sita was caged part of the time to keep her still. The tail stopped wagging, the bounce left her, and her eyes were sad. It almost killed me, too. Wherever I went, people asked where she was. Even strangers, who approached me at the Y, at the restaurants, the post office, and at church asking about her.

I am convinced she had a purpose. She rallied and came back better than anyone ever thought. She is much older now and tires easily. I decided to have her go with me part of the day but not all day because it is too hard for her. She works for me part time, and we go out every single day. I know to be at home and not to go out with me ever would be depressing because all she has known for ten years is how to help me. She takes slower and easier walks, stopping frequently to rest. She is content to be in front of my apartment sniffing the grass and being the mascot for the entire neighborhood as adults and children both stop to pet her and rub her belly.

Sita goes over once a week to see Max. They no longer play, but they sit together in a comfortable silence. She no longer flies to other states with me but takes shorter trips to hotels for a couple of days. People are still happy to see her, and the light is back in her soulful, beautiful eyes. Her tail is wagging again, and the bounce is in her step. I think of all we have been through together.

Ecclesiastes 3:4 states it best, "There is a time to weep and a time to laugh, a time to mourn and a time to dance."

It is amazing to me how life goes full circle. Many times it happens in the smallest ways. Some people call these coincidences, but I prefer to call them God moments.

I was visiting a college friend in Springfield where Sita had been abandoned in the streets. We have great times together as we stay up late and laugh and talk and giggle. She attends fundraisers at Circle

Tail with me. We go out to eat, go to church, and visit with her many friends. I went to her school when she was teaching and did a program for her students. When she comes to visit me and we talk, laugh, and giggle all over again! It is the special friendship of someone I have known for over forty years.

On this particular visit, we decided to go to a local winery near her home. When we walked in, I realized this was a dog's paradise. There were dog wine holders, figurines, and even special wines named after some of the rescue dogs in the area. It was obvious that the owners did a lot for dog rescue. They had a huge jar where patrons could donate and proudly told me that yearly they held a huge benefit to sponsor a local shelter.

Chills ran down my spine as I realized the shelter was Clark County, the place where Sita had been rescued. I told them she was one of their dogs, and they, too, were surprised.

I gave them my book about Sita. They took several pictures to share with the shelter. The shelter has changed for the better and is now a no-kill place. I even met the woman who'd rescued Sita and called Circle Tail. She remembered Sita very well and was working for another rescue place!

Was this coincidence? I do not think so. I think this was a God moment. Ten years after her rescue, Sita was in the winery sponsoring the place where she'd been found. Wow!

Sita and I have done so many things together and still are. We were meant to be together, and I will always be grateful for this wonderful dog that changed my life, and the lives of many others, forever.

"Where can I go from Your Spirit? Where can I flee from Your presence? If I go up to the heavens, You are there; if I make my bed in the depths, You are there. If I rise on the wings of the dawn, if I settle on the far side of the sea, even there Your hand will guide me; Your right hand will hold me fast."

PSALM 139: 7-10

Dear God,

I sometimes despair and do not understand why certain events happen, such as someone abandoning a gorgeous dog like Sita. Let me understand that You always have a bigger and better plan for all your creatures including me.

Amen.

About the Author

Jane Biehl, Ph.D. has had several exciting careers as a librarian, counselor, college instructor, and writer. She holds master's degrees in library science and rehabilitation counseling as well as a doctorate in counseling. She resides in North Canton, Ohio, with her hearing-ear dog, Sita, and an ornery rescue cat, Cesar.

Jane is profoundly deaf and has worked with hard-of-hearing and deaf persons all her life. She passionately writes about dogs, hearing loss, and, as a cancer survivor, how to kick cancer's butt, having published many articles and several books on these topics including a picture book for children titled *Here to Bump and Bump to Hear*. Additionally, Jane has delivered compelling presentations at several national conventions as well as locally for Circle Tail, the organization that introduced her to Sita, and One of a Kind Pet Rescue, where she found Cesar.

In her free time, Jane can be found reading, participating in her book club, following all Cleveland sports teams, trying new restaurants with friends, and traveling just about anywhere. She's an active member of the Congregational United Church of Christ Church and Aultman Cancer Center advisory councils.

Jane and Sita have been partnered since 2007 and, according to Jane, are lost without each other.

Made in the USA
Columbia, SC
02 April 2018